Wallace P Stanley

Our Week Afloat

Or, how we explored the Pequonset River

Wallace P Stanley

Our Week Afloat
Or, how we explored the Pequonset River

ISBN/EAN: 9783337240653

Printed in Europe, USA, Canada, Australia, Japan

Cover: Foto ©Andreas Hilbeck / pixelio.de

More available books at **www.hansebooks.com**

I SPREAD THE UMBRELLA AND SAT ON THE FLOOR OF THE BOAT.
SEE PAGE 28.

OUR WEEK AFLOAT;

OR,

HOW WE EXPLORED THE PEQUONSET RIVER.

BY
WALLACE P. STANLEY.

WITH ILLUSTRATIONS BY HENRY N. CADY.

CHICAGO:
BELFORD-CLARKE CO.
1891.

W. B. CONKEY CO., PRINTERS AND BINDERS, CHICAGO.

LIST OF ILLUSTRATIONS.

I Spread the Umbrella and Sat on the Floor of the Boat,	Frontispiece

	PAGE.
A Fellow Leaning on the Rail Fishing,	111
A Little One-Story House,	165
A Scow was Lying Close in to the Shore and They were Heaping Hay on It,	361
As Pretty a View as We had Seen that Day,	73
Every Few Moments a Frog Would Let Himself Off,	92
He Landed Near the Bottom of the Slope,	97
"Hello!" I Cried, "Here's Somebody's Anchor!"	312
Here's Something That Doesn't Need Winding Up,	161
Indian Pipe,	183
It Lifted Me 'most Out of My Shoes,	158
It was a Queer Looking Affair for a Mill,	211
It was Curious to Watch the Changes in the Lighted Space Just Ahead of Us,	341
It was 'most as Heavy as Our Mast,	277
Joe Picked Up a Couple of Stones,	206
Joe Sprang Out From the Edge,	97
Joe Went Overboard With a Slump,	101
Night Hawks were Sailing and Plunging Far Above,	261
Nobody at Home To-day, I Should Say, Remarked Joe,	251
"Now," Cried Joe; and We Brought Down the Sticks With All Our Force,	355
Our Two Little White Houses,	85
Pews Free,	230
Playing "Tens,"	272
The Boundary Stone,	34

LIST OF ILLUSTRATIONS.

	PAGE.
THE CHANNEL WENT RIGHT OFF AT RIGHT ANGLES,	63
THE OLD MAN TURNED AND SURVEYED US,	23
THE OLD ORCHARD,	243
THE RAFT WAS HARDLY BUOYANT ENOUGH FOR TWO,	297
THE SEA,	32
THE SMALLEST FERRY-BOAT ON RECORD,	69
THE SPRING,	119
THE WATER POURED INTO THE BUCKETS AND THE WHEEL BEGAN TO TURN SLOWLY,	237
'TWAS A BIG SNAPPING TURTLE,	324
'TWAS A PRETTY RESPECTABLE CAVERN, THOUGH, TO LOOK AT FROM THE OUTSIDE,	187
'TWAS FULL OF MOSSY STONES, WITH BIG ROCKS CROWDING IN,	231
'TWAS WONDERFUL HOW HIS HEAD PLUNGED OUT.	326
THERE WERE FACES, TOO,	285
WE BOTH LAID HOLD OF THE PAINTER; AND AFTER THE START SHE SLID ALONG LIKE A SLED,	47
WE BROUGHT THE BOAT INTO THE COVE,	115
WE EACH GRABBED A HANDLE OF THE BIG BAG,	19
WE LOOKED LIKE DROWNED RATS,	281
WE'LL HAUL HER OVER,	39
WHEN WE CAME TO A BEND HE'D CALL "PORT" OR "STARBOARD,"	127

OUR WEEK AFLOAT;

OR,

HOW WE EXPLORED THE PEQUONSET RIVER.

CHAPTER I.

We didn't know it was the Pequonset River when we set out to explore it. You see, it was the upper part of Pierhaven River, which wasn't really a river at all, but an arm of Mattaconsett Bay. It ran up about two miles from the bay, then came the town of Pierhaven, on the east side; and there it was about a quarter of a mile across.

Just above the town it narrowed; and this was where the bridges went across — first the carriage bridge; then, a little further north, the railway bridge with its heavy truss-timbers Then it spread out again, wider than ever, but pretty shallow, except in the channel, and ran up a couple of miles further to Wylie's bridge, and beyond here it was a different thing altogether — only a few yards wide, and winding about like any up-country river; but its water was still salt, and the current ran six hours up and six hours down, according to the tide. It was a strong current, too; it went past the wharves as fast as one could walk, and it was no light job to pull a boat against it.

But we knew that far above Wylie's bridge, in regions remote and unknown to us, there were a mill-dam, a pond, and an old cotton-mill — one of the oldest in the country. This was the "Clermont Mill"; but we had always heard it spoken of as "Shad Factory," because the shad had to stop at that dam when they ran up from the bay in the spring.

Now, we had a boat, Joe Thurston and I; in fact, we have her yet; but the time I speak of, early last summer, we had owned her less than six weeks. She was a flat-bottomed skiff, thirteen feet long; we were glad to pay Tom Rollins five dollars each for her; for, after two years in his service, she was still as staunch as ever.

The *Triton*, as we called her, was not famed as a fast boat; but, by each taking an oar, we could get up a speed which suited us very well, especially if wind and tide were favorable. Then, however, we usually left off rowing, and raised our sail, a sprit-rigged affair, too small to be of much use in going to windward; but, with a good breeze on the quarter, it would carry us at a pretty fair rate.

By the time we were well posted in the *Triton's* ways — had fished from her for "scup" at Sauket Point, and for "tautog" near the bridges; had gone clamming at Upton's Bend, and crabbing around Bowers' Island; and had skirted all the shores on both sides within two or three miles of our landing-place — the summer vacation set in, and with more time on our hands, we began to think of lengthening our trips.

It was Joe who proposed that we should camp out for a few days on "Slade's Island," some distance above the bridges. Some fishermen made their home there every spring, while the shad were running, so as to look out for their nets near by; and no doubt this gave Joe his idea. I was well enough pleased with the notion, and went to look at the county map.

I always like to have a map when I go anywhere. You can see how far you've got, and what there is ahead of you, and can judge to what point you can go, and get back by dark; you see where the cross-roads will bring you out, where you can cut off, and whether you can go home by some other way. I had half-a-dozen little maps all traced; one of the Wensdale turnpike and the connecting roads, another of the country toward Pocannoc Hill, and so on; so all I had to do when I went on a tramp, was to tuck the map of the region I was going over into my pocket, and I was all right. I had found some things, too, and marked them down, that weren't on the printed one.

But, though the map-makers got the roads and other inland things about as they were, it seemed to me that they were rather careless when they came to the shore. They would fix on some long point, and mark that down in its place, and then measure off, and put down another a mile or so away;— and they seemed to wiggle their pencils along anyhow for the part that came between. I suppose they were in a hurry and thought it didn't matter,— and it *doesn't* matter for Pierhaven River; for Joe and I fixed all that.

Of course I traced it off the big map, as soon as we got the boat; and there's a good deal to it, what with wide places and narrow places, bends, branches and islands. Well, as you might know, we kept finding that where the water notched in a little, it wouldn't be set down; and where the land rounded out a little, they'd have it go straight; but, as I was saying, we attended to all those places; and we put down where the bottom was sandy, and where there was eel-grass, the gravelly shores and muddy shores, and the good places to dig clams and catch fiddler-crabs, and the springs of fresh water, and everything that was of any use; so that I had hard work to print fine enough to get it all on; and then, I tell you, we had a regular chart that was worth something.

We hadn't paid much attention yet to the region above the bridges; for one thing, it wasn't easy to get there and back, with the tide rushing and roaring between the piers, except at slack water; and then there wasn't anything particular to draw us there. You could see eel-grass trailing along the surface almost all over it at low tide; and it was the cruising-ground of the "mud-fleet," a squadron of scows, square at both ends and decked all over, so that they were nothing more than floating platforms; the crew raked the eel-grass off the bottom and piled it on the scows till it was as high as their heads, and the deck was almost under water; then they carried it ashore and sold it to farmers by the cord for manure. The shores were flat and covered with salt-grass and scrubby undergrowth; and altogether it seemed somehow dull and stagnant compared with the river below the bridges, with its clear, deep water, crisp waves, and brisk currents.

These things came into my mind, as my eyes ran along the outlines of the river, to nearly the top of the map; and I felt less interested in the prospect that Joe's words had opened. It came to me that the camping out was really the important thing, and "Slade's Island" of little account.

Joe had followed me, of course; and we both looked at the upper part, where lay the island, and where, further up, the river suddenly narrowed, before it was crossed by Wylie's bridge. Just at this point the State line slanted across, and then everything stopped short, as though it was the end of the world. It was tantalizing.

"Joe," said I, "do you know anything about what there is up beyond?"

"They say that you come to 'Shad Factory,' a good ways up; and I saw the same that you did, when we walked through Pine Woods and around over Wylie's Bridge, last fall."

We had seen the river winding from side to side of a broad stretch of low meadows covered with coarse salt-grass, extending like a valley between rising ground and trees; behind which its further course was hidden about half a mile north.

"And you never heard how far the river goes, or where it comes from?"

"No."

"Well, Joe, it's for us to find out."

CHAPTER II.

It seemed to be thought a rather odd and unheard-of freak, this sudden fancy of ours for going exploring into parts unknown;—but there couldn't much fault be found with it, after all. Nobody could well expect us to be drowned up in that brook, after we had been voyaging about on the river for weeks past; there were no savages, or even wild beasts,—more's the pity,—and it wasn't likely to be enough of a wilderness to amount to anything; there would always be some farmer's house within a mile or so. The worst that was likely to happen was exposure to wet weather, and for that we had long rubber coats. It was summertime, and we were tolerably rugged chaps, each past his fifteenth year.

Besides making various preparations for our expedition, we had to take the tide into account, before setting a day for the start. Of course, we wanted to set out on the beginning of the flood, so as to have the current in our favor all the way up to Wylie's bridge, and as far beyond as it could make itself felt against the fresh-water stream; and if the tide was ebbing in the morning, we couldn't start till towards noon, and the first day would be only half a day.

But it turned out very well for us; for by the time we were ready, the tide was out late in the afternoon, and consequently early in the morning, also; and it was just time for new moon, by all the almanacs.

So one morning, when July was nearly half through, Joe and I were astir by daylight. I lived nearest the water, so the sail and oars were kept in our woodshed, and they were as much as I cared to tackle for the first load; for we had three oars,— a seven-foot pair and another short one to steer with, as it controlled the boat so much better than a rudder.

Now three oars are rather awkward things to carry with one arm; you have to look out and keep them lapped and balanced just about so, or they'll slip and kick out crossways, and act as contrary as if they meant it. But I was used to their tricks, and dumped them all right at the landing-place in two minutes' time.

There was our little *Triton* waiting for us, that was to be our home for a week or more, and take us into places we knew nothing about;— mysterious and unexplored regions, I liked to imagine they were; and they were so to us, anyway. I loosened the stern mooring line, and hauled her in to the ladder by the painter. The tide was so low that when I stepped aboard, she touched bottom; she was paved all over with big drops of dew, but there wasn't a particle of salt water in her; Joe and I had spent half a day caulking, and we did it up in good shape. I took the sponge from the locker, and wiped her off.

When I went up to get the oars, there was Joe starting down the wharf, lugging along a tremendous traveling-bag covered with black waterproof cloth; just as I caught sight of him he stopped to change hands. He took off his hat and gave it a swing.

"How's tide?" he sung out.

"Chock low!" I answered. In a minute more he set his bag down on the cap-log, and wiped his face.

"Where shall I check it to?" I asked.

"Sources of the Pierhaven River! Just heft it."

"Well, it'll be lighter when we come back"; and I tied the end of the painter to it, while Joe went down the ladder. I lowered him the bag, and the other things; and when he had stowed them away I fastened the painter, and we went up home for the rest of our cargo.

No one else was on the street; but we heard one or two window-blinds bang, and saw the smoke curling out of the chimneys all around. The sunbeams were just poking through the gold-colored clouds and slanting across the roofs, making the windows flash as though they were afire.

"I wonder where we'll see the sun rise to-morrow!" said Joe.

"That's so!" said I.

A couple of carpenters turned the corner, carrying their tools and smoking their pipes; barely glancing at us as they strode by. They didn't know they had met an exploring expedition!

I had started the fire when I first came down; and now our good-natured old "Peggy" was bustling about the kitchen.

"An' the great voyagin' travelers is goin' to start! It's a foine day ye have. Will ye be stayin' to breakfast?"

"No," said I, "it's 'most five o'clock, and we must be off. Come, on, Joe, and help fill the jug."

"Well,— but hold on," said Joe. "We don't know just how long we'll be gone; and we might as well save taking anything out of the bags this morning. The tide hasn't turned yet."

Joe had caught sight of the smoking griddle; and I knew he liked hot flapjacks.

"I'll have the cakes all hot for yez in wan minit."

I didn't feel as though I wanted to eat anything at all; but I saw there was some sense in what Joe had said, so we sat right down at the kitchen table; and when I had once begun I got along very well. And Joe! I wish I had kept count of his flapjacks, but I didn't think of it till too late.

I had bought a bag like Joe's,— he had his before,— and it was just the thing. I had crowded it out even bigger than Joe's, but then he was there

WE EACH GRABBED A HANDLE OF THE BIG BAG.

to help tote it. We filled the jug,— it wasn't a very big one, for we were going to sail on fresh water,— and then I went to get the blankets.

We each grabbed a handle of the big bag; Joe picked up the jug with his other hand, while I carried a tin kettle crammed full of things, and a big umbrella; and each of us had a rolled-up blanket tucked under his arm. We staggered off, trying to keep step; and Peggy called out of the window, "A pleasant voyage and safe return to yez!"

We were afraid some of our fellows might happen along and "guy" us; but the only one we met was old Captain Eldridge; and he laughed and said, "Movin' day, is it?" and we said, "Yes, sir;" and trudged right along. When we turned down toward the wharf, we felt it was no use trying to put it straight through; so we let everything down, and took a halt.

"My arms ache fit for four!" said Joe. "Wish I *had* four, about now!"

"Well," said I, "the *Triton* 'll carry all these, and us besides, for miles and miles."

"Maybe," returned Joe; "but I reckon we'll have done a good stiff pile of rowing by that time."

We found the tide was beginning to come in; and we hurried things aboard, and cast off in short order. There wasn't any too much room in the *Triton*, with such a load; but there was room enough; and we each took an oar, and pulled away for the channel.

My! but wasn't it lovely! The sun shone bright and hot, but the air was cool and crisp, with a little breeze; just enough to crinkle up the reflections of the houses and trees, and set them all a-shimmering;—and there was that delightful salty smell that comes from the kelp and sea-weed when the tide is out.

There was Jake Bisbee, pushing his chubby boat around Bowers' Island, looking for crabs; and we were glad of a chance to yell.

"Hello-o-o! what luck?"

The old man turned and surveyed us, with his spear half-raised.

"Middlin'— Going fishin'?"

"We're going exploring!" I shouted.

"Goin' which?"

"Yes, we're going fishing!" called out Joe. "Among other things," he added, in a lower tone.

We passed the island, and the upper wharves, where lay a couple of coal-schooners and the *Sylph*, an old white tow-boat which wandered about the bay, and now and then appeared in our river, and began to draw near to the bridges. We saw, as we expected, that the current was still flowing down toward us from them;—and yet we had certainly just seen that the water was slowly creeping up the stones of the wharf.

THE OLD MAN TURNED AND SURVEYED US.

CHAPTER III.

You see, it was this way: The passage at the bridges was narrow, considering the size of the river above and below; and during ebb the outflow from above could not keep pace with the withdrawal of water from the lower side; and the difference of level between the surface above and below kept growing greater, till at low water it amounted to several feet, so that the current rushed down between the piers, with quite a savage roaring, boiling, and splashing; there were not many who cared to "shoot" it in a small boat at such times.

Then, when the tide began to "come in," it would have to rise for some time, before meeting the water above the bridges on the same level; and meanwhile the downward flow would keep on, though growing less rapid as the tide rose. Of course, it followed from all this that the rise and fall on the shores was decidedly less above the bridges than below.

We found the current tolerably gentle, and made up our minds to pull through against it; for it would soon turn, and the earlier we got by, the longer the tide would favor us on our way up.

"I'll send her through," said Joe.

"All right," and I gave him my oar, stepped to

the stern; and shipped the steering-oar; for in the narrow space between the piers the stream would "slew" the bow around "in no time," if she wasn't pointed straight.

The bridge stood on three stone piers, making four openings; over the westernmost of which was the wheel-house of the tide-mill. The railroad bridge went across a few rods further north.

I made for the opening between the two eastern piers. Joe urged us on without much trouble till within twenty feet of the bridge; then came the tug. He instinctively pulled harder, to keep up the speed.

"Don't strain yourself, or you'll give out; just pull easy, and you'll fetch it; we're gaining."

Joe relaxed from his spurt; and we did still gain, but slowly enough; we seemed to make only two or three inches a stroke. "I'm good for half an hour, at this rate!" he declared.

The shadow of the bridge fell across the bow; it crept along over the bags and came marching across Joe's hat. He pulled just right; calmly and steadily as a steam-engine. The shade mounted to my knees,— we were fairly under.

"I like this," said he; "it's more comfortable out of the sun."

The smooth black water slid beneath us with a gentle rippling noise, and gurgled against the piers on either side; the left rowlock kept giving out a little squeak, as regularly as a clock.

Suddenly came the loud hollow thump and rattle of a team, on the boards right over our heads; it rumbled away over the other arches and was gone.

Now the sunlight struck on the forward end. "'Most through, Joe!"

"If I *must* come out of the shade, I'll pitch in!" he said; and with half-a-dozen mighty strokes we were through. This was more than half the battle; for the piers of the railroad bridge were fewer and further apart, and the current, having freer course, was more gentle. In less than two minutes we were fairly beyond the bridges.

"Now I'll spell you and give you a chance to rest," and I took the oars, while Joe sat in the stern and mopped himself.

In ten minutes' more pulling, we had made such progress that the roar of the six o'clock train, as it crossed the river on its way to the city, came over the water with a muffled and distant sound, which made the stillness seem greater than ever when it had gone by. The light northerly air had at last dropped away altogether, and the surface was like glass, except for the double row of curdling circles which narrowed off in our wake.

I was gazing dreamily at some seaweed-rakers, away to the east, and thinking it was going to be a pretty hot day, when suddenly there was a faint rustling beneath, and the next stroke was as if pulled in molasses.

"Where're you steering to? you've run us into the eel-grass!"

"That's so! I wasn't looking for it so soon. We can't be far from the channel," and he stood up to take a survey. "I see it! Back her out;—fetch a stroke or two with your starboard oar,—now give way!" and presently we were in a sort of lane of clear water, on either side of which the eel-grass dotted the surface as far as we could see. Near by, the long, slimy, yellowish-green ribbons were in sight, lying in a closely-packed mass, and all pointing straight down stream as smoothly as though they had been combed. Now and then a big bluish-green crab, sunning himself cosily on the top, would scuttle away into the depths as we went by.

"What time is it?" I asked.

Joe drew forth his Waterbury watch, and answered, "Twelve minutes past. I'll take the oars again at quarter past."

He had not been rowing long, when dark bands of ripple began shifting over the river behind us, and we soon felt a refreshing little puff from the south.

"Let's spread the sail," said Joe.

There wasn't enough wind to give us much headway; but my next turn at the oars would be due in a little while, and I had no objections to make to Joe's proposal. The mast was shipped and the sprit dropped into the "snotter"; the sheet was belayed, and we slipped noiselessly along up the the channel.

The breeze was so light and fitful that the sail kept dropping inboard; so Joe took an oar and "boomed out" the after clew. Then he began to rearrange things. We had adjusted the forward thwart so it could be easily taken out; he now lifted it from its bearings and wedged it across with the edge upward, so that it braced the blankets which he stowed against it and the side of the boat in such fashion as to make quite a passable lounging place. Then he settled down with his hat off and his head in the shade of the sail, looking as comfortable as a cat loaded with a full charge of cream.

I spread the old umbrella, and sat on the floor of the boat, with my arm resting on the locker; and along we drifted, not more than three-fourths awake. I don't suppose we were a very ship-shape looking crew; but none of the fellows were there to make remarks, and we never pretended to man-of-war style, anyway.

After half-an-hour or so of this, we got into a long, straight stretch of channel; and I was sleepily watching the little eddies curling away in our wake, when all at once the breeze began to freshen. The umbrella, which I had let go of, rolled over and nearly went overboard, while the oar dropped from the sail and fell into the boat with a whang and a rattle; making Joe jump, and then look very wide-awake and indifferent.

"Wake up, Joe, and bear a hand!" I laughed, "the old ship'll weather it yet!"

"Wake up yourself!" he returned, "and take a reef in that old parachute. There's Slade's island, on the lee bow," he continued. "We're 'most half way to Wylie's bridge. I'll take the helm, if you like."

So I took possession of the lair in the bow, and readjusted the blankets to fit my own particular sprawl.

The wind was still only moderate; and presently I had an idea.

"We'll rig out a spinnaker, and go wing-and-wing!" and I picked up the big umbrella, which Joe had disdained, and unfurled it once more to the breeze, securing it with twine at the port side so as to balance the one-sided pull of the sail. Now the strain on the steering-oar was eased, and we rippled along at a pretty good rate.

CHAPTER IV.

The river was about half-a-mile wide. On the west side stretched the dense, dark-green "Pine Woods," which came nearer to the idea of a forest than anything else within reach of our tramps; it was pleasant there, too, with the clean brown needles underfoot, and no underbrush to scrape through; and in some places there were lots of wintergreen leaves and berries. There was not a house to be seen; and on the east side, which was a good deal further from where we were, there were only a few roofs, here and there; it seemed to be mostly oak and hickory woods. The steeples were small and dim, far away to the south; and all around, the eel-grass kept the water still as a duck-pond.

"You wouldn't think, to see it now," said I, "that so many big ships had come down through here."

"I believe you!" said Joe. "I wish they had kept it up long enough for us to have seen it."

We were born just too late to know much about Rodman Brewster's ship-yard except by hearsay. We knew that it lay just southwest of Wylie's bridge, with the Pine Woods at its back; and that in the old whaling days it had sent ship after ship to be fitted out at the Pierhaven wharves,—from which they sailed away to the very ends of the earth. Over a hundred and thirty vessels had been launched from that yard.

It did seem strange to think of those big sea-going craft first taking the water away up here in

THE SEA.

the country, where it seemed like a land-locked pond. There were two ship-yards down at Pierhaven and they were busy right along for a good many years; but the biggest ship that ever sailed from that port—the *Sea*, of 900 tons—was built at Brewster's yard.

Wouldn't I like to have seen her! coming slowly down on the top of the flood-tide, towering tall and black, with no ballast or cargo to weight her down,—tugged along by row-boats, and sticking fast in the mud at ebb. It took several days to get her down to Pierhaven.

After awhile the shores began to draw nearer together, and Wylie's Bridge was in plain sight, not more than a quarter of a mile away.

"Say good bye to New Jersey, Joe," said I; "the line runs across about here."

"I wonder if that isn't the boundary stone?" said Joe, pointing ahead.

There was a post on the eastern shore, some distance off; but we couldn't be sure whether it was wood or stone. It might be nothing more than an ordinary mooring post.

"Just take the helm a minute, and I'll soon find out," and Joe opened his bag, and after a little rummaging, produced a small red leather case, which I knew held his pocket spy-glass. It might better be called a single-barreled opera-glass; as it was made on that plan, having only two lenses; and, of course, it was not a very powerful instrument; but it was equal to this occasion.

"It is the boundary stone," he exclaimed, and he handed the glass to me.

There it stood, a few feet above the high-water mark; a square stone post, looking almost white against the background of bayberry bushes and scrub oaks. The river had narrowed so rapidly that the shores at this point were only a few rods apart;—and in less than two minutes we furled the umbrella and unshipped the sprit, and the *Triton's* bow was run ashore opposite the landmark.

THE BOUNDARY STONE.

When ever boys come across a boundary stone, they have to stand astride of the line ; and, of course, that is what we did, trying to realize to the full the proud sensation of standing in two States at once.

Then we reëmbarked; and, leaving our native territory, pushed away for the unexplored wilds to the north.

This spot, however, looked as peaceful and commonplace as possible; with the square white cupola of a little country church on the right, and a few quiet old houses grouped around among the trees; and it was not unknown to Joe and me, we having walked around past here by land, as I have said.

On the left was the site of the old ship-yard, and the large old-fashioned mansion of the master-builder, further back, across the road.

In front, and close by, was the bridge; and after unshipping the mast, Joe took the oars again, and pulled her through. It was quite a different job from that at the first bridge. We could see that there was a very slow current in the direction we were going.

We were now in a different region altogether. It was no longer like a big pond; but it wasn't much like a river, either. It seemed more like a deep, wide ditch, than anything else, except that it kept crooking. The tide being low, there were the muddy banks rising a yard above the water on either hand, with a tall crop of salt-grass on the top; so that as we sat on the boat, we could see nothing but the short stretch of water before and behind. When we stood up, we could see the flat valley of bright green, waving grass, extending north for two or three miles.

"Do you suppose it's fresh yet?" inquired Joe.

"Not very likely, I should think; the shore 'round here looks pretty salty."

"Yes; but the tide's out, and this water must have come from a good way up. I'll try it, anyway!"

So he scooped up a cupful; but he didn't swallow much.

"Agh!" he said, "I'd rather have it clear salt than this stuff."

"Never mind," I told him, "there's plenty in the jug."

The jug had been in the shade, up in the "forepeak," as we called it; and we both found it as good as we wanted.

"You thought to change the cork, this time," observed Joe.

"You better believe!" said I.

The jug had once been used for vinegar; and the first time I carried fresh water in it, when we made a voyage down the river, one Saturday, the same old vinegar stopple was left in; so when we came to drink, the water "tasted" just enough to ruin it;—but we were so thirsty, that we had to drink nearly all of it, to stop our drought; though I'd 'most as lief have taken medicine — some kinds I'd rather.

CHAPTER V.

I picked up the oars again; and after rowing easterly a few rods, we rounded a bend, and another stretch opened, leading north-west.

"It'll be dull work, rowing around all these bends; we'll have to go three miles to make one. Let's shake out the sail again," I proposed.

We had the wind free up that reach, and made fair progress; though the bank partly becalmed the lower part of the sail; but pretty soon we came to the next turn, which curved sharply, and ran a little to the south of east, bringing the wind forward of the beam. The *Triton* didn't make very good headway now; and though her flat side held her some, she made enough leeway to get jammed up against the north bank in a minute or so.

We dropped the sprit, and rowed to the next bend; and then the sail carried us up again for quite a long stretch. Then came a turn which led right back again in the direction from which we had just come; but it was a short one. I drew the oar inboard.

"You shove her through this, Joe; and I'll gather in the sail."

So I went forward and held the sail folded up against the mast so it wouldn't hinder us, and Joe took an oar and thrust it against the bottom,— 'twasn't much over three feet deep,— and fetched us through with about a dozen shoves. Then I let the sail spread again, and up we went.

We kept on in this way for some time; sailing when we could, and pushing when we had to. On two or three long crosswise stretches, we took to the oars. Now and then we would stand up on the thwarts to see what our prospects were around the next bend.

"There's getting to be a sameness about this," said Joe.

"Yes," I assented, "but anyway, we've discovered the crookedest river *I* ever was on."

We came to a place where the stream turned and stretched off eastwardly for quite a distance. Just ahead of us a fence was built down into the water; Joe stood up and took a look.

"Gracious!" he exclaimed, "this beats anything yet."

So I got up and looked too; and it did. For when the water got through with its easterly stretch, it swept around in a great half-circle, and came back again toward us; and that fence went down again into it fifteen or twenty steps from where we were. I never saw so little fencing do for so much land; that big peninsula—"almost an island" it was indeed,— must have amounted to six or seven acres.

"Isn't it mean!" said Joe.

"Yes! and we'll have to row both ways," I added.

The sail was flapping loosely; and, drifting sideways, we brought up gently against the shore.

"We shan't row either way!" suddenly asserted Joe, "we'll haul her over!"

"Of course we will!" I cried. "Joe, you're inspired. But let's lighten her, first."

We pushed her to the other side of the fence, where the bank was more shelving, and took out the bags, the sail and oars, and the jug, which we put in the shade of a tree near by. Though this place was not as steep as most others, we had a hard tug to get her up on the level.

Joe laid hold of the painter, while I took off shoes and stockings, and pushed at the stern; we hitched her up sideways, first one end, then the other. When we got her up, we took off our hats and sat down under the trees a little while.

"I don't know but it's harder work than it would have been to row around," said Joe.

"May be 'tis," I answered, "but it breaks up the sameness. And there is a deal in that." But I think the best of it was, that we had somehow outwitted the "knurly" old river.

"You're not getting tired of exploring yet, are you, Joe?"

"Not a bit! but I feel like exploring the lunch-bag more than anything else, just now. But we'll put her over first."

The rest of the job didn't amount to very much; we slid her across the smooth grass in short order, and launched her, bow foremost, leaving her after part ashore for the time being. Then we sat down by the bags and took account of our stock.

There were plenty of hard-boiled eggs, of course, and I had some pieces of huckleberry pie, cut so as to roughly fit a tin kettle; these were overlaid with slices of cake, the lower layers of which were streaked a beautiful purple by the huckleberry juice; but they were all the better for that, to be sure;

then there were cookies and doughnuts, and Joe had a dozen corned-beef sandwiches and some extra slices of the beef in a box by itself. From these viands we tapered off, through cheese and milk-crackers to hard "pilot-bread," or "hard-tack," as we called it, of course. Then I had a can of salmon, all the way from Oregon.

I hardly need say that we didn't expect these stores to last us a week or more; but our vision of penetrating the unknown wilds was underlaid by a solid faith in the unceasing neighborhood of farmhouses, with all the abundance of good things which it is their business to supply. Besides, we had our fish-lines along, though neither of us was very expert in fresh-water fishing.

We agreed that we had better begin with the more perishable things, and put them out of harm's way; so we set to on the pie and sandwiches, and had quite a feast.

Across the valley from us was a pasture-lot, with an old white horse cropping at the grass and swishing away the flies. Near the middle stood a big sycamore, or "buttonwood"; most of the smaller limbs were broken off, and there were only half-a-dozen green boughs on the whole tree.

Every such forlorn-looking old stager in this region, within two or three miles of salt water, has a fish-hawk's nest on it,—sometimes two. This had one; a big one, near the top.

Joe got out his spy-glass and we took a look at the nest. We couldn't make out whether there was anything in it; it was just a great rough pile of sticks and dead branches, enough to fill a cart — same as they all are. It must be a deal of work to build such a pile of a nest; a robin's would have to be as large as a peck measure to be in the same proportion.

Joe and I began discussing whether a fish-hawk's nest always killed the tree, or whether they took a tree which had begun to decay of its own accord. I thought, the last; because the sycamores in that region are all more or less blighted. It was hard to be sure, as they live in the same nest year after year; and I never saw a freshly-built one.

At last we saw a fish-hawk — or osprey, as it is also called — flapping along from the south; and it was easy to see it had a fish. Joe clapped the glass to his eye.

"It's alive!" he declared, "I can see it wriggle!"

"What kind is it? Let's see,"— but when I took the glass the bird had nearly reached its nest, and what caught my eye were some little heads stretched above the edge;— and in a moment the fish was among them, and they were out of sight again.

"Seems to me a fish-hawk has a rather hard life," said I. "I'd rather be some other kind of bird."

"Oh, they're not so badly off. Nobody troubles them, and they're used to their work."

"Maybe so; but when it comes to sousing under water in all weathers, and lugging a heavy fish for miles,——"

"You'd rather sit still and reach your hand into the bag!"

"Just so — nothing like being contented with one's lot."

CHAPTER VI.

When we embarked, we found that the water had risen two or three inches, and that the *Triton* would have floated off by herself in a few minutes more.

" Do you see? there's an up-current," I said.

" So there is ;—a pretty slow crawl, though."

" Yes; but the tide isn't full at Pierhaven 'till eleven ; and it 'll keep coming up here for some time after that. I shouldn't wonder if it helped us a good deal yet."

We went on about half an hour, around bends and " ox-bows" of all sizes and directions. The water rose fast ; it was nearly level with the bank in many places. You see, there was quite a stream of fresh water coming down from above all the time, and the rise of the tide dammed it up, so to speak ; where we were it was filling up from each way.

We had been looking out for another chance to cut off, but without finding one narrow enough to be worth trying. At last I thought I saw a place that would do.

The neck, or isthmus of this peninsula, was ten times as wide as the one we had hauled across ; but the bend was bigger, too ; and we could cut off a deal. But the main point was, that the neck lay so low that it was all "awash,"— on the side where we were, at any rate. The grass rose a foot or more; but close by we could see the water shining all in among the stalks; and it seemed to me there was enough for us to slip her through easily.

My shoes and stockings were still off, and I said I would wade across and see. It was rather queer walking, splashing along through the thick grass; but there was water all the way, ankle-deep in some places.

So Joe's shoes and stockings came off too. We didn't undertake to lighten the boat; the trouble of carrying the things by hand that distance would amount to more than their weight aboard would cause her.

We both laid hold of the painter; and after the start she slid along like a sled; the sail was up, taking the wind; and that helped some. Anybody a little way off would have thought we were hauling her over dry land. She smoothed the grass down like a flat-iron; when the farm hands came to mow they must have wondered who left *that* trail.

When we were nearly across we noticed an old grindstone at one side on higher ground, under a low-spreading oak; and we said we'd keep that in mind for a landmark to know that cut-off again; for most of those bends down there were surprisingly alike.

Where we took to the water again, there was a long straight northward stretch; I jumped aboard, Joe gave her a good shove-off and grabbed the steering-oar, and we skimmed along gaily.

The water had become quite brown; we couldn't see the bottom at all. When we got around the next bend I asked Joe to sound; he jabbed the oar down, but it was deeper than he allowed for, and it floated up without touching. He drew up and gave another dig, and this time he struck it; but he had to reach his hand under water to do it. It was a seven-foot oar.

"Tell you what," said I; "next time we come up, we'll charter Ed. Serrell's sloop, and bring all the fellows.

" Hello — ship ahoy!" cried Joe; "here's your vessel, now, right ahead."

I looked; sure enough, there was some kind of a big red craft about a quarter of a mile off, with a few men polling it slowly along; it had just come in sight from behind a row of willows.

"I know what it is," went on Joe; " it's a brick-scow! that red is bricks. That's why the Sylph was lying at Burrill's Wharf this morning."

And Joe proceeded to get out his spy-glass once more; but there was no need. I knew as well as Joe that there was a brick-yard up this way somewhere, and that every now and then deeply-laden scows appeared at Pierhaven bridge, which were

WE BOTH LAID HOLD OF THE PAINTER; AND AFTER THE START SHE SLID ALONG LIKE A SLED.

towed away to various ports on the bay by the queer old side-wheel tug-boat.

In half a minute more another could be seen pushing out from behind the willows. They made pretty slow progress; but then, the current, such as it was, was against them.

We came nearer by degrees, sometimes going the same way, sometimes contrary, according to the bends; and when at last we got into the same reach, we saw there wasn't room to pass, for they kept squarely in the middle. So we hauled the *Triton* up ashore, and waited for them to pole by. One of the men hailed us:

"Where're you from? Wylie's Bridge?"

"We're from Pierhaven."

"Must have started early."

Another called out, "The Sylph got there yet?"

"We saw her this morning."

"Hear that?" he said to the others. "Old Cap'n Jotham'll jaw us for not loading up in time to get down there yesterday!"

When the other scow came along, there was a boy perched on top of the bricks, which were piled up quite neatly, with a place left all around the edge of the scow, for the men to walk on. He had on faded blue overalls, with one suspender; and looked at us without saying anything. I called out: "How far is it to the brick-yard?"

"Dunno," said he.

"'Bout a mile, by water," said one of the men. "Goin' fishin'?"

"Perhaps so; any fish up this way?"

"Not much, I guess. Some shad gets up here in the spring, but they're through runnin' long ago."

"There's bull-pouts in Harlow's Pond!" the boy woke up enough to say. "And you might find punkin'-seed in some places along up!" he called out, as the scow moved off.

"Bull-pouts! punkin'-seed!" I repeated. 'What's he giving us?"

"That's what they call catfish sometimes,— bull-pouts, or bull-heads," explained Joe. He had gone fishing with his cousins in Connecticut, and knew more about fresh water than I did. "And I've heard of punkin'-seed; but I don't know exactly what they are."

We pushed off the boat, and continued our voyage. The valley through which the river wound was not as wide now, and the bends were shorter; the salt-marsh grass had given place to the ordinary meadow kinds, and the trees were growing close to the water, here and there. Before long we came to a long row of willows, growing close together at the water's edge, where we had first seen the scows. They shaded us, and that was pleasant enough; but at the same time they took the wind from the sail.

But Joe went to sculling with his steering-oar, and we forged onward as fast as we cared to. We weren't in so much of a hurry, now that we were out of that tiresome salt-marsh region.

Just after passing the willows, I noticed a plant growing out of the water, close to the bank; it had a few large arrow-head-shaped leaves, and among them was a stalk with a short green spike at either end, dotted over with little blue flowers.

"That's a pickerel-weed," said Joe. "We're clear out of salt water now, I guess. You might take a taste."

"Don't care to try again, eh?" I rejoined.

The water was rather warm, and its flavor wasn't very choice; but there was no salt about it this time.

The shore kept rising now on the west side, till it was quite a bluff; now and then an old worm-fence came zig-zagging down to the water, with a line of trees and bushes alongside of it; and the trees began to come gathering along the river-bank.

The sail was of hardly any use: so I took it down and rolled it around the mast, and stowed it in the boat. Then I took up the oars and pulled slowly along.

It was quite a change for the *Triton*,— this sort of thing. She was used to dancing and dipping across the big waves in the channel at Pierhaven, when the tide was flowing down against the southwest wind ; and to grounding on gravelly beaches where the little breakers rocked her about among the kelp and sea-wrack ; but to be gliding on a fresh-water stream away up inland, with the grass and leaves dipping into the water on either hand, was something new for her,— and for us, too. And, for a change, we liked it very well.

CHAPTER VII.

After a time the bluff on the west became quite steep, and jutted out in a sort of promontory covered with a grove of oaks, almost black except in spots near the top where the shiny leaves sparkled in the sun.

Here was quite a bend to the east; and beyond, on the other side, a flat tongue of land ran out, with an immense willow on it, overhanging the water. Some cows were standing knee-deep under the willow, with the sun mottling their sides where it shone between the leaves.

The cows didn't seem to mind at all, as we drifted down to them, but stood working their jaws and swinging their tails.

"I wonder if they'll wait till we charge into them," said Joe.

But as we drew nearer, we saw that there was room for the boat to get by in the deep channel under the west bank. Still I thought it best to draw the port oar inboard.

All of a sudden Joe reached down for the old umbrella, and opened it with a rattling flap,—and gracious! what a plunging and splashing! They sent the water all over us, and made the *Triton* wabble about as though she was in a "sea-way" again.

. The beasts floundered up ashore, and bulged their eyes out at us. I couldn't help laughing, though I was nearest and took most of the spattering.

"Come, Joe! you might have got us upset! Suppose one of them had been a bull!"

"I wish there had!" he exclaimed. "I'd like nothing better. Think of him roaring and ripping after us! We'd keep in the channel, and watch him swim. He'd come from off the bank, and charge sideways at us! I'd like to see him,— wouldn't I just set this oar-blade 'tween his horns!"

But I thought it just as well that Joe's bragging wasn't put to the test. Before we were out of sight, the cows had straggled back into the water again.

"There's the brick-yard!"

I turned, and saw some long unpainted sheds, and a smaller brick building, with an outside factory chimney, standing on bare yellow ground, east of the river. There didn't seem to be anything going on, except at the water side, where a few men had nearly finished loading another scow. They stood in a line, a little apart from each other; a man at one end was on the scow, the others led off to the heap of bricks, up on the bank.

It was fun to watch them, they managed it so neatly. The one at the shore end would pick up four or five bricks at once,— ranged in a pile one above another, and toss them to the next; and so they were pitched right along, till the last man got them, and laid them on the scow. By that time two or three more bunches had started from the shore end; they kept it up as regularly as machinery.

It wouldn't do for one to get behindhand, for the bricks were in the air most of the time; and it seemed wonderful that the bunches stuck together so well. I suppose they *must* drop, sometimes; but they didn't while we were looking at them.

The river widened out a bit, here, and we got by without any trouble; the men barely glanced at us, without speaking.

"They want to get down to Pierhaven to-day," said Joe.

Under the sheds were heaps of unburned bricks, piled loosely in "kilns," with spaces for the smoke to escape. On the further side was a long row of boxes or trays, where the clay and sand were stirred up together with water by machinery; but as the works weren't going, we didn't care to stop.

Before long a bend hid the place, and we were alone again. Down below, in the meadows, we could see quite a distance up and down the course of the river; but here the trees grew along the bank so closely that often we could see little more than the reach we were in. But for all that, it was pleasanter; every bend showed us a fresh view, that we had never seen before. Now we began to feel really like explorers.

All at once, as we rounded a curve, the water in front was split by a point of rocks, with grass and a few junipers on top; this point widened rapidly as it went further up, and rose, too, with good-sized trees springing from it. The river had branched!

"That's bad!" I said, "we won't have so much road to travel in!"

"We'll take the main stream, anyhow," said Joe.

But which was it? The branches seemed to be about equal in size. The one to the left had a high, rocky bank, which went straight down into the water, in some places; the other was a little wider, with a somewhat shelving, gravelly bank on the right, and rocky on the other, or the end of the point. But in this the water was flowing slowly,—still upward; while in the left, it seemed to be at a standstill. Besides, the right fork was rather more in a line with the direction below the point; so we decided to take that one.

When we got in we found it was so shallow that we could see the bottom plainly,—rugged and rocky, and colored in various deep shades of brown. Joe sounded, and found the water less than a yard deep. The current was brisker than it had been yet, but as it helped us, that was all right.

As I rowed along I noticed a number of dark-colored shells scattered on the bottom, near the shore.

I brought up the boat, reached over and picked some up.

They were about the size and shape of a clam, but colored like a mussel;—they were fresh-water clams. I had seen some shells of the same kind in cousin Albert's cabinet, brought from the Ottawa River, in Canada.

"Let's get up a clam-bake!" said I. " Do you suppose they are fit to eat?"

"Nothing like trying!" said Joe.

Now raw salt-water clams are not as good as cooked ones; still they are eatable,—at least, hungry boys have thought so more than once. So I cut one open. It looked rather queer, but it was plainly a clam; so I took a bite.

Poh! there was't any taste to it! It was just toughness, and nothing else; a piece of wet rubber'd be about as good. It was unnatural and disgusting that a clam should have no sort of savor.

"Not quite right, eh!" laughed Joe.

"I hope they're better cooked! But I don't think I want to try them again, in any shape. It would take an alligator to chew 'em and an ostrich to digest 'em!"

So I tossed the lot overboard, and pulled ahead.

"They're not rightly clams, they're mussels," said Joe. "Clams burrow; these don't."

But as far as flavor went, I thought the salt-water

mussels were as much insulted as the clams, by the comparison.

"Why didn't you hunt them for pearls?" he went on. "It's been proved that one fresh-water mussel in every hundred has a pearl, and of every ten pearls there's one big enough to be worth something."

"I'm rowing," I replied. "Why don't you take up the business?"

But the clams had nothing more to fear from us.

Our branch now began to turn to the left; and the bank on that side became lower. Then, after a long, straight stretch, the course turned to the right again. At the next bend, the bank on the left doubled around in another point, and there was still another branch making off on the other side of it!

"Confound this river!" exclaimed Joe. "It's all splitting up! I wonder which is the right one, *now?*" for the forks, as before, were of about the same size.

"Let's see what the course is," said I, "I'm all turned 'round."

I got out the compass, and we found that the branch on the right led off about north-east, while the other stretched away a little south of west.

"I think this river comes down in a northerly direction," said I.

"So it does, in general; but we've boxed the compass a dozen times already since we left Wylie's bridge. Each of these may turn the other way in the next five rods. We want to take the one that's got the most water."

"Of course."

"Well, that's the one!" pointing to the left. "Just watch that leaf!"

It was a yellow hickory leaf, fallen before its time, and curled up at the edge just enough to make a first-class fairy canoe. Though there was no wind at that place, the bushes being thick, it was moving, slowly but surely—moving toward the junction.

"See!" said Joe. "In the other fork, the tide's going up still; but in this, there's fresh water enough coming down from above to set the leaf down stream."

There was no denying it,—here was at last the first trace of a downward current. Without more delay, Joe swung his helm, or his oar-handle, to starboard; and we entered the fork. The leaf which had guided us narrowly escaped being run down; but it glided by unharmed, and I watched it swirling and dancing merrily away in our wake.

CHAPTER VIII.

Our river soon grew quite narrow, with steep, rocky banks on either hand. I had to draw the oar-handles inboard past each other, to get room to row.

"Sorry it's getting so narrow; we'll have to depend on sculling, pretty soon."

Joe sounded with an oar, but could hardly reach bottom.

"That's good; there's plenty of water," he said, "it'll widen out before long."

But though it grew no wider, it grew deeper. The rocks almost straight up, on either side, to more than twenty feet above the water. It was a regular little *cañon*.

Above, the trees arched over thickly, all glimmering with spots of bright yellow-green, where the sun struck through the leaves, as they shook in the wind; while the birds hopped about chirping and the locusts buzzed.

Down where we were it was cool and shady, and the splashing of the oars sounded hollow and echoing, like a bucket in a well; the rocks were damp, and green with moss in some places, and dark and glistening in others, where little sheets of water ran down from cracks, and tinkled into the stream.

I wonder if the old *Triton* knew who she was, in such a place as that!

The course curved a little, and opened up a new vista, a closed one; for a wall of rock stood right across the further end. At the same time, we heard a low murmur of rushing water.

"No thoroughfare!" said Joe.

"Your main channel did'nt last very long;" I observed. "We'll have to back out through; I don't believe there's room to turn 'round."

"Hold on!" said he, "let's go to the end. We both saw there was a current; you can see it's coming down against us, yet;— and don't you hear the water running somewhere ahead?"

"I know," said I, "it goes through a tunnel under the rocks, Joe. We'd have rigged up some diving apparatus if we'd known we'd got to explore under water."

A few strokes brought us to the end, and it was no end at all! The channel went right off, at right angles, to the left!

I was never more surprised; and I guess Joe was just as much. We backed off again, to take a look from where we first saw it, and now we could tell where the break was; but we never could have made it out before.

Well, then we turned the corner; and the noise of rushing water kept growing louder; the passage turned a little, and there it was! a water-fall foaming down the rocks from nearly three times as high as my head. There wasn't very much water — about twice as much as you'd pour from a good-sized bucket, only it kept coming all the time, of course; and it spread out, and rushed over the notches and steps of the rock, and made as much show and noise as it could; and it was right pretty to look at. It was pleasant, too, to come on it suddenly, without expecting it, as though we were the first discoverers; and there was nothing to show we weren't.

We stopped and looked at it a while; and then we began to think of getting by. The rock must have sloped down towards the edge, for the fall started off with quite a curve-out; and though most of it hit the rocks part way down, there was one spout that made a clear leap out into the water at the bottom, and there was a deal of spattering.

"Let's get under the umbrella!" said I.

But Joe pooh-poohed that, and said all it was good for was to scare cows. "It'll be more fun to 'run the gauntlet;' it can't amount to much, anyway."

So we backed to the turn, and then put on steam and came tearing down, with Joe thrusting against the rocks with his oar from the stern; and we travelled through the spray in a second. It wasn't equal by half to the splashing I got from the cows. So then we went on, with the fall sounding fainter

THE CHANNEL WENT RIGHT OFF AT RIGHT ANGLES.

and fainter; presently we turned to the left, and lost sight of it. The rocks on each side began to be lower; we were coming to the end of the cañon.

"There she widens!" cried Joe.

"Good!" said I; and I put a little more vim into my pulling; for I was tired of being so cramped for space.

"Well! Great Cæsar and pig-iron!" roared Joe.

What do you think? there where the river widened was still another branch forking in, nearly in the same direction in which we had been coming; and, strangest of all, the branch was fully as large as the main stream we were on; and yet, after dividing, the river seemed larger than ever; as large, in fact, as it was before forking the first time!

"It's an enchanted river!" exclaimed Joe. "The more she splits up, the larger she grows!"

"Well, bring on your surprises!" said I, "you can't astonish me any more!"

But that wasn't so. We looked up around the new branch; and Joe clapped his hand on my knee, but for a few moments neither of us said anything. We *couldn't* say anything that would come up to it!

We knew that rocky point, and those junipers; we had seen them within an hour. We had been circumnavigating an island!

CHAPTER IX.

Where we saw the leaf, the branch which at the first forking passed off to the left, united with the other to form one stream again. No wonder the current flowed toward the junction.

"Well, Joe," said I, "it seems there was water enough in that branch to take us down stream; but I shouldn't wonder if the leaf was traveling up, still!"

"If you knew better than I, why didn't you say so!" snapped Joe.

"Oh, come now, what's the use of getting mad? Of course I thought the same as you did; and after all, you wouldn't want to have missed seeing that cañon! it's the best exploring we've done yet. 'Twas a fortunate mistake, Joe!"

So he let down his bristles; but he said he'd keep his eye open for islands, after this.

We worked back again up the right side, for that was easier rowing; but it was rather dull going over the same ground again. Where I had stopped to pick up the clams there was a dozen minnows tugging and fighting over the one I had cut open; but nothing bigger.

At last we came to our second forks, and it seemed plain enough now; but Joe insisted on stopping and piling up a little heap of stones on the point, with a stick built among them pointing out towards the passage we had just come through.

"We're likely enough to hit more such places; and I'll make sure of this one."

Then I gave him the oars, and we began once more to make progress into parts unknown.

We hadn't gone a dozen boat-lengths, when there was the identical leaf, floating along up as calmly as ever. Joe gave a dig at it; but we were too far ahead, and it bobbed away serenely. As I told him it wasn't the leaf's fault, but ours who didn't understand it.

Now we came to a place where our course wound about through pastures and meadow-lots for quite a ways; and there weren't many trees near the water, so that we could see the bends ahead, as we did below the brick-yard. It didn't make big oxbows, and come doubling backward as it did there, but went crooking along in an average northwesterly direction.

The meadows sloped gently away, and we could see as much as half a mile in some places; and then the view was stopped by stone walls, with thick, low apple-trees on the other side ; or by barns and other wood-colored shanties such as they always have—corn-cribs, hen-houses, and what-not—stringing along till you come to a well-sweep sticking up against the sky; and there's the house, with a long flap of roof running down to one story high towards the meadows; while on the other side, toward the road along the ridge, it shows two stories.

There were three or four houses in sight; and they had little bits of narrow windows spotted here and there on the gables, and dormer windows making dots of shadow on the roofs, like old eyes half-shut and sleepy; but the sleepiest things were the roofs themselves, stretching along under the trees, and gleaming bright and still in the afternoon sunshine.

There were no signs of life but the little white dots of chickens creeping about. Now and then we could hear a dog "wuffing" a long way off.

All at once we rounded right into a school of ducks; they raised an outrageous quacking, and Joe was startled almost as much as they were. He had been rowing with his eyes shut, and I don't believe he was more than half awake.

The ducks marched away, solemnly shaking their tails, as though they disapproved of that sort of thing.

"They're not used to boats," said Joe, "I haven't seen one on the river yet."

"Except the brick scows."

But we came on one, right away. It was where a fence came down to the water on each side, and a path ran along by the fence. A little square tub of a boat was moored there, just big enough to hold one person; it was fastened to a line which ran

around a pulley at the top of a stake, then across the river and around another pulley on that side; then it went back across to the boat again. A man coming either way could get in the boat, and pull himself across.

"It's a ferry-boat!"

"Yes the smallest on record," said Joe, as he lifted the rope over his head. "I'd like to see Buster Williams cross in that!"

As "Buster" "tipped the scales" at 240, it isn't likely he would have been willing to try.

A horse lay under a tree in the lot we now came upon; he struggled up and came slowly down to investigate us. He was a sober and venerable-looking old nag, and he stretched his neck wistfully after us, as though he would like to come aboard and take a ride.

After zig-zagging around a while among the pasture-lots, we coursed along the edge of a grove of oaks which covered the slope to our left, and sheltered us from the sun; which was getting low enough to be a little uncomfortable. I don't mind the sun half so much in the middle of the day, for then your hat-brim can shade you, if it's decent-sized; but earlier or later it edges around underneath, and you can't keep out of its way.

Before we passed by the grove, we agreed to land and open the bags again. We laid in so much piecrust before, it was some time before we got hungry again; it was now nearly three o'clock.

So we sat down in the shade and ate; and then we wandered about a little, to stretch our legs. I started a chipmunk; and we watched him capering about and chattering at us — which brought another — and they both followed after us, jumping from tree to tree. We "spotted" acorns at them; but they didn't seem to mind.

It was four o'clock when we started again; and after a few minutes' rowing, we came in sight of a bridge about a quarter of a mile ahead, — the fourth since starting.

It was a solid-looking stone bridge, with one arch, and some tall trees on each bank beyond, through which we could see some roofs on the right, and some blue smoke curling out of a chimney. The half-circle of the bridge was repeated in the water, among the dark reflections of the trees; and the whole made as pretty a view as we had seen that day.

Soon we were splashing through under the cool arch. Beyond, the river widened out to twice its ordinary size; there was a large, low, rambling house not far from the water-side, and a big stone barn a little further off. There was a veranda along the front, overrun with vines, where a girl was sewing, with a dog lying beside her.

When he heard our oars, he jumped up and came

AS PRETTY A VIEW AS WE HAD SEEN THAT DAY.

bounding to the shore, where he ran up and down, barking at us; he was a big, good-natured looking fellow, and the girl tried to call him back, but he wouldn't mind; I didn't know but he'd jump in after us, he was so excited.

A little further along, a handsome row-boat was moored to the bank; "Kittie Clover" was painted on its stern. A little boy and girl were in it; they had been fishing, but now they were too much taken up with looking at us to pay attention to anything else.

We rowed up and asked if they had caught anything. The boy held up a string of four or five minnows.

"Not enough yet for a chowder," remarked Joe.

Then I asked how far it was to "Shad Factory." They didn't seem to know; but the girl had come down by this time, and got the dog quiet; and she said it was about eight miles. She didn't know how far it was by water. "How far is it to where the current begins to run down?"

"It's generally running down *here*," she said. "At full and new moon it runs up part of the time; the tide from below crowds it up. It was running up here an hour ago."

It was dead still now, as far as we could make out. But we couldn't expect it to stay so long; and the further we got before it turned against us the better. So we thanked her, and pulled away

We turned to the right, and lost sight of the bridge, and its pleasant neighborhood. The river became narrower again, but still we noticed no current.

By and by it widened out again, and made quite a pond; ten times our boat's length across, and much longer than that, up and down. On our right was a pretty steep hill, with a flock of sheep nibbling over it; towards the top, some rocky ledges cropped out, and still further up were thick woods.

On the other side, a number of large willows were growing close to the water. Then meadows stretched back, with several oak and elm trees, and orchards; a few farm buildings in sight, and a white church-spire beyond, with its vane gleaming in the sunshine like a star.

I don't think there are any trees handsomer than willows, take it altogether; especially when the sun is low, and lights them up the way it did then;—they are big, solid, and grand-looking, and still so light and cheerful, with the fine feathery leaves, all silvery on the outside, and warm and mellow on the inside, where the sun strikes right through and touches up the orange-colored twigs and switches; while the big boughs go forking up among it almost black, except where the light straggles through and brings out cinnamon spots, here and there.

And it grows, all over; the leaves and twigs cover it down to the ground; and it branches right away;

no tall, stiff trunk. It's a domestic kind of a tree; you don't find it on mountains and in "trackless forests," but along pleasant stretches of water like this, with men's homes not far off.

The wind had died down, and the water was still, so that everything was doubled;—and it was worth being doubled. I told Joe to stop rowing a little, so as not to shake it up.

He thought it was lovely, too, He said it looked as though there might be fish there; and we said we'd try for 'em on the way back.

Then I got out an oar astern, and sculled slowly along through it. Where it narrowed, there was a shoal bank of gravel on the side toward the hill, that ran out half-way across. We went right along over it, in about a foot of water, with the bottom paved with stones of all shades of deep orange-red and brown.

And in a minute we saw, and no mistake, that there was a current down-stream. Not much of a current, but it was there.

"The salt water's helped us as far as it can, this time," said I, "and it's a deal further than I expected."

"Yes; it'll be up-hill work, after this."

But there was no difference to notice, yet; and when, in the course of a few yards, we got off the shoals, it was next to nothing.

CHAPTER X.

So on we went; and after a while we came to a patch of woods, mostly oaks, with some pines and birches. It seemed like twilight in there, and we hurried to get out of it; for we wanted to pitch our first camp before the daylight gave out.

The woods didn't seem pleasant for camping; the trees were pretty close together, and there was lots of underbrush; it looked damp and swampy, too; and the mosquitoes squealed their finespun tunes about our ears. We each took an oar, and pulled away at a good rate; partly to get away from them, and partly to get out of the woods before dark; for we didn't know how large they might be.

Fortunately, the stream didn't crook very badly in here; as it was, we bumped her nose into the bank at two of the bends; and at last I took the bow oar, and made shift to row facing forward; then I could look out for the direction.

It seemed as though we kept at it that way for an hour and a half; but it was only a little over three-quarters by the watch. Then we saw the trees thinner ahead, and presently came out on a wide sweep of meadow, with a herd of cows standing and mooing around a gate in the further corner on the other side of the gate, a lane led to a barn some distance away. That pasture was well cropped; 'twas no wonder the beasts were ready for supper.

It didn't seem so late, now; for the sun was no longer shut out from us; we knew, of course, it didn't set till after seven, but we didn't know, till we found out for ourselves, how long the river staid in those woods.

I took my oar to the stern, and Joe pulled along easily. After we passed the meadow, there was an orchard on the left, with plenty of apples; but they were too green for even a boy to eat. Then we came to quite a high, steep hill, with gray rocks cropping out, here and there; dozens of juniper, or "savin" trees, of all sizes, were growing around and among the rocks.

This hill rose up right in front of us; but the river didn't run over it; that may be the way of roads, but not of rivers. It curved off to the east, along the base.

Soon after we turned there was a sort of bumping scrape along the bottom ; enough to startle us a little, but it did no harm. We knew what it was; one of the rocks from the hill had got into the river, and rose almost to the top; I could see it plainly enough as soon as we had scratched over it.

"We must remember this place, Joe; if the water had been an inch or two lower, we wouldn't have got off so easily."

"Better keep your eye peeled for another," said he.

We coasted around the hill to its eastern slope, when the stream turned to the north again. On our left rose the rocks and junipers; it was quite a steep and rugged ascent here, and it cast a long shadow to the eastward, over a sort of scrubby pasture,—patches of grass, mixed up with huckleberry bushes and clumps of "bay-berry" or wax-myrtle, and groups of stunted oaks and junipers.

We could see there were plenty of berries on the bushes; and I brought her up to the bank a few moments, while Joe jumped ashore and cut off some of the thickest loaded ones, which he threw into the boat.

In due time the hill rounded off to the west and the river curved in the same direction; but now it did not hug the base quite so closely. Now the trees in the pasture grew quite thick and woody, but only for a little while; presently they all stopped at an old stone fence, and here was a long stretch of green meadow, with the sun glinting across, and the river making two or three bends through it, before it slipped into a clump of willows on the further side.

A little way ahead was a washout on the hill-side, where the storms had laid bare the sand and gravel, which had spread away down to the water, making a rounded, sandy point, around which the channel curved; here the river was quite narrow, but beyond it widened out, making a little lake.

There was a decided current in the narrows, enough to slow us up some; but when we got through into the pond, so bright and clear, with little dimplings here and there, where the water-beetles were darting and whirling about, and the green turf sloping down into it from the hillside,— "Here's the place for us to camp!" cried Joe, and as for me, I was just going to say the same.

CHAPTER XI.

We pulled the *Triton* up half-way ashore, and bundled out our things. We slipped the sail off the mast; then we took the sprit and made one end of it fast to the mast at the top; we shipped the mast, and lashed one of the oars to it, about two feet up.

Then we lashed the other end of the oar to the lower end of the sprit and carried the cord down on each side of the cleats in the boat, where the sheet was belayed in sailing; this kept the oar steady lengthwise in the middle of the boat. Thus we had a sort of figure-four arrangement.

Then we unrolled one of the blankets, took out the "cot" which was wrapped up inside, and unfolded it. This was made of stout "drilling," with a cord sewn in around the edge, like a sail; it was cut to fit the shape of the boat,—wider at one end than the other.

The *Triton* had a good sized "fender-strake" around the gunwale; into the under side of it I had driven round-headed brass screws, five on each side of the forward part of the boat; the heads were left sticking out a little. There were five loops on each side of the cot, at distances to match; so we only had to button the loops over the screw-heads, and the cot was slung securely across the boat; reaching from the main thwart to the little forward deck where the mast was shipped. Of course we took out the forward thwart; you see now why we had made it removable.

Now we took the sail—which was to be a tent over night,—and threw it across the oar, which was the ridge-pole. The "head" or top of the sail, being narrower than the foot, we brought up against the mast, where the boat was narrower, after drawing it down smoothly on each side, we tacked it along the fender. It lapped over some, up forward, but there was'nt much to spare, where the boat widened out.

Then we spread the blanket over the cot, and there was a bed and shelter at short notice. It looked snug enough; altogether two snug for two, but of course we knew that beforehand; and we had brought along the means for rigging another shelter.

We went up a few steps from the water, and drove down four stakes which we had brought with us, so that they stood at the corners of a space three by six feet. In the other blanket was another cot, the sides of which were folded over so as to make a wide hem, of a size to fit the oars, which we ran in just as the stick is run in at the bottom of a window shade. Part of the oars stuck out at each end, so that we could lash them at the top of the stakes.

Then we drove two longer stakes opposite the

middle of the head and foot, with a line stretched between the top ends for the ridge-pole ; this line was brought down from the stakes to pins in the ground, so the tent shouldn't sag; the other stakes were secured in the same way.

This time, the tent was not adapted, like the sail, but made expressly for the purpose ; with flaps which could fold across each end and button, to keep the wind off. It had holes at each corner, worked with "button-hole stitch," and through these we tied it to the stakes, and pinned the edges to the cot, along the oars. Then we spread the blanket inside, and our camp was pitched.

But all was not complete, yet. There was a small roll made up of four pieces of mosquito-netting; these we fastened with safety-pins across both ends of each tent; lapping and folding so as to make all tight against the little sharp-nosed intruders.

Now we stood off and looked, and we felt pretty proud. There, where half-an-hour before, there was nothing, were our two little white houses all built. We could hardly wait till dark to try them;—it was our first camping-out, you know.

Then we had to find out "which was to have which;" and Joe took off his hat.

"Now, who'll have the boat!" and he slung it high in the air.

"Sing out which you'll have !"

"Heads!" said I.

OUR TWO LITTLE WHITE HOUSES.

It came down on the sail, and rolled off on the farther side; and when we went around, it was crown up. If we'd cared, we might have said it wasn't fair; but we didn't care, so I was to have the boat.

Then we said we'd go up on the hill and eat supper, and fill our pillows. These were nothing but bags fixed to button across the mouth; we were going to fill them with leaves.

So up we went; and it was worth while going up to get the view. We could see glimpses of the river here and there, a long way down to the south, and could make out the salt meadows we had come through that morning; and with Joe's little glass we thought we could see the causeway over which the road led to Wylie's bridge. A clump of big trees rose up a good way off, and covered where we thought the bridge ought to be.

But one thing we were sure of — the Pierhaven spires. Nobody who was ever brought up under those steeples could mistake them. They were as small as could be to show at all, twinkling away off on the horizon; but the glass cleared them up enough to leave no doubt. Below them we could see a little gleam of the river below Wylie's bridge

"We're in sight of home still!" said Joe.

"Yes; but we've come a pretty long way to-day, around all those bends."

"Farther than we'll go any other day," said he.

"We've got the current to reckon with from this time on."

We faced round to the north to see what we were coming to; but couldn't make out much. We could see the river in only two places, after it left the meadow below us, and those were within a mile; so we thought it must run among woods more than it had yet.

But we could see spaces of open country, too; and some hills, two or three miles off, higher than the one we were on, for they reached above the horizon line.

The meadow, below us, was almost all in shade; but the river, reflecting the sky, looked brighter than ever, and the sun struck across the tops of the willows beyond.

There lay our little tents, at the water's edge,— how very little and lonely they looked! And yet that was home to us, for to-night.

"Just think, Joe!" said I, "that's the same boat that lay at the wharf this morning. We didn't have the least idea then how the place would look where we are now."

"Well, now we know; and it's a pretty, pleasant place. I'd rather be here than there; and so would most of the fellows, I guess!"

"So they would. They're coming home, about now, from fishing or tramping, or playing around the wharves; but I don't believe many of them have had as good a time as we."

"I guess most of them are at supper, by this time," remarked Joe, "and I move we follow suit."

So we sat down on some smooth rocks; and the bountiful bags swung open again

Looking eastwardly we could see several houses about a mile off; they seemed to be arranged in line as though along a road, making a little settlement, and there was a white church tower, or cupola, a rather queer affair, as we saw it through the glass, "like a drum on a soap-box," said Joe.

"Wouldn't this be a prime place for a fort against the Indians!" he went on. "Here's the river on three sides; and if they *did* get across, we could pepper 'em to pieces before they'd scrambled half-way up this steep slope. Just run a stone wall between a dozen of these biggest rocks 'round here, and we'd be ready for the whole tribe of 'em!"

"That sounds very well;" said I, "but if you saw a gang of red-skins skipping across that huckleberry pasture, all painted up, and yelling to you to 'hold the fort, for they were coming,' how you'd streak it for——"

"Not a bit; I'm politer than that. I'd treat 'em on pie and hard-tack, and swap our blankets for a whole boat-load of furs; we'd go back rich!"

"Well, then, I'm glad they're not coming; for I want that other piece of pie myself!"

We had brought our huckleberry-bushes with us; and when we shut the bags, we took them and sauntered around, picking and eating as we walked. The sun had now gone down, and the sky was mostly clear; but some long, slate-colored clouds lay low down along the west, with red streaks between; and above them some light filmy yellow streamers went sweeping up, and higher still were bars of what we called "mackerel-sky," dappled white and gray,—but the proper name is cirrus-cloud; so the books say.

We picked our bushes clean; and then Joe was for going down.

"It's getting dark, and I'm plum tired."

"Wait a minute," I told him, "we haven't filled the pillows."

We went and got out the bags, and carried them to a good-sized bayberry bush on the south slope. Bayberry leaves were just the thing for that;— small and clean, and not juicy so they'd mash up,— and they smell good, too.

While we were stuffing our bags, the west blazed out bright again; the streamers and mackerel-sky were all orange-red and rose-color,— just lovely.

"That's good for us!" said Joe, "it means fine weather."

Then it turned dull and gray, and we plodded down to our camp. While we were undressing, the mosquitoes tickled about some; but as we were fixed for them, that was all the better. There's no comfort in being secure, if there's nothing to be secure against.

I tucked my clothes in the locker at the stern, and Joe found room to stow his at the lower corner of his cot, which was bigger than mine. He crawled in, and called to me to pin the mosquito netting again, where he got through.

I told him that would never do. "You'll be locked in, and I can't have you yelling to me to let you out, at any outrageous hour you may happen to fancy!"

But I held it for him while he pinned it from inside. "How is it?"

"First-class!" said he; "as easy as a hammock!"

He bagged it down to within two or three inches of the ground; but an inch was as good as a mile. There wasn't any wind, so he left the flaps at the foot wide open; at the head he fastened the lower buttons, leaving a hole at the peak.

I went down and sat on the stern, rinsing my feet in the water; then lifted the netting and floundered in. How cosy it seemed! and plenty big enough, too: and this was the little white speck I had seen from the hill-top, with the great world stretching far away around it. A warm, dim, creamy light came through the sides of the tent. In front was a three-cornered bit of light-gray sky, above a dark mass of trees blending into the meadow; then a watery gleam close by.

The crickets were chirping their best; and every few moments a frog would let himself off, now near, now further off. I could see nothing of Joe or his tent, I seemed entirely alone, but it was just jolly! except, perhaps——

"Say!" I heard Joe call out.

"What!" I called back, putting my face to the small opening above my head, where the peak of of the sail folded around the mast.

"Aren't these blankets fearfully scratchy?

"I was just thinking I wished they were a little smoother," I replied. "I'm afraid we're not up to roughing it yet."

"There's no need of it!" said he, "I'm going to put on my drawers."

This was a good idea, and I acted on it; but I had to crawl out, again, to get at the stern-locker. It was getting pretty dark now and cooler. The boards of the boat were damp with dew. I couldn't see Joe, in the shade of his tent; but I could hear him well enough.

"Suppose you should slink off before I was up! wouldn't I be in a pretty fix! you've got all the stores aboard. But I'd have your scalp, sooner or later!"

"Never mind about what you'd do; I want you along to help row. If you want any security, I'll bundle the bags in with you!"

"No, thanks. What'll you do if the tide rises?" he went on. "Have you moored her?"

We had thrown out our little grapnel, as usual, on landing; and it seemed to me that was enough.

"No fear about the tides getting up as far as this!" said I.

"But if there should be a freshet? a good solid thunder-storm might raise the stream a foot or two."

"Wouldn't I laugh if it did!" I cried. "You'd wake up nice and cool! I'd ride as safe as Noah's ark, while you'd be floundering like herring in a seine! But I'd want to be on hand to see, so I guess I'll tie up."

So I took the painter and fastened it to one of his cot stakes. "I'll tie it around your ankle, if you're afraid of my giving you the slip." But he guessed the stake would do.

Then I got in again; it seemed nice and warm, and the blanket didn't scratch now. Pretty soon it seemed rather too warm, but I knew it would be cooler toward morning, and didn't think it best to throw off the blanket.

Then I remembered that I was a little thirsty, and had meant to take a drink when I was out before, but forgot it after all. I was wide awake enough, but hated to take the trouble to go out once more; and I must have gone to sleep while I was trying to make up my mind about it. I've noticed that before — there's nothing 'll put you to sleep quicker than to think of something not *very* important, but something which *perhaps* you ought to get out and attend to.

CHAPTER XII.

I was awakened by a tremendous splashing, and at first couldn't make out where I was, or what was the matter,— then I saw it was Joe, kicking about in the water in front of me.

"Hurrah!" he shouted, "come on in, and wash your eyes open!"

"Well, quit splashing into the boat, and I'll see!" and I crawled out, half awake, and shivering in the chilly morning air.

"Come on!" cried Joe, again, "the water's warmer than the air!"

"It might be," said I, "and still not be very warm!"

"It's a splendid sandy bottom!" he went on, and he plunged across to the deeper part, and struck out up-stream.

But he was more of a water dog than I; and after washing my face and neck, and taking the drink postponed from the evening before, I proceeded to get into my clothes.

Joe shortly came ashore, and also began to dress.

"How long have you been up?" I inquired.

"'Bout quarter of an hour. How'd you sleep?"

"Slept right through; did you?"

"Not quite; I woke up a little after two;— a

mosquito did it, I think; one was in, anyhow; and I found where he got in, too; where the cot sagged away from the netting. I fixed that; and it wasn't long before I was off again. It was dark, then, I tell you;— cloudy all over; I was afraid 'twould be bad to-day, for all that sunset. But it's come out all right."

The sun was just rising, among broken gold-gray clouds; overhead it was clear, but hazy lower down. A light, cool breeze from the north was rippling the little pond.

"So you didn't forget to wind up that Waterbury?"

"No, but I came near it; I thought of it just after I spoke to you last. When I woke up all I had to do was to strike a match, and there was the time. I couldn't have had any idea without it, and no stars showing."

We ate a little, so as not to work on an empty stomach, and then "struck camp"—rigged the sail on the mast again, and bundled the stakes together; but the cots and blankets were just a trifle damp, and we spread them out on some rocks facing the sun. We went up on the hill again, but it was rather misty, and we could not see as far as on the evening before. The view looked quite differently, with the light coming from the other way; and we saw houses to the westward which we hadn't noticed before.

"Well, we're fairly started in for explorers!" said Joe. "I wonder where we'll stop to-night."

"It won't be as different from this place as this is from where we were the night before. We ought to pass 'Shad Factory' to-day."

"Yes; I only hope we won't get to the head of navigation! But there won't be much of a river left by the time we do that."

We strolled along to the top of the washout, and looked down aslope of sand as high as a house and as steep as the roof; lower down it grew less steep, and by the time it spread into the water it was almost level.

All of a sudden Joe skipped back about a rod, then came down with a rush, and sprang far out from the edge. He landed near the bottom of the slope, pitching in half-way to his knees, then plunged down, sand and all, three or four yards farther.

"Come on! it's just gay!" he shouted.

So then I jumped. We tried it about twenty times; and I never saw a better place for a sand-jump. We were in the air long enough to know it, and wish it would last longer. I'd like to jump a hundred feet, if it wasn't for the "stoppin' so quick!" as the Irishman said.

But the scrambling up again was tiresome work, and the sun was getting hotter and hotter; so we went where our bedding was spread out, and found it was dry as a bone. Then we loaded it aboard, and moved away from the spot where we had passed the night. All that was left to show that a party of explorers had camped there was half-a-dozen stake holes, and the track where the *Triton* had been drawn up. There weren't even the charred remains of a fire.

"It's the first camp I ever heard of that didn't have a fire," said Joe. "We ought to have started up one so as to be in style."

"No; make a style of our own, I say; we had nothing to cook; we don't drink tea or coffee, and we were warm enough. It would only have drawn the mosquitos."

"We ought to name the camp, anyhow."

"All right; name ahead."

"Well, let's see, — Camp — Camp Huckleberry."

"Talk about style!" I laughed.

"Well, I didn't really mean that; but there's nothing else in particular about the place that I know of, unless you call it 'Camp Washout.'"

"Pshaw! yes, there is. We got the widest view from that hill, that we've seen, so far. Let's call it Camp Prospect." And Camp Prospect it was.

By this time we had pulled through the little pond and were in the current. Joe had the oars: I'd handled them more than he, the day before.

"But take notice," said he, one mile of pulling to-day 'll be equal to at least three of yesterday's!"

After the willows had cut off our view of Camp Prospect, we went for quite a while through a swampy sort of region, where the clumps of underbrush came down to the water, and kept us from seeing very far. Once we heard a rattle of an ox-team, and the driver singing out to them now and then but we could see nothing; and soon they were out of hearing.

Sometimes the bushes and small trees grew right out of the water, on each side; and all along they swept the surface with their leaves, so that in a good many places you couldn't see where the land began. The wind seemed to have gone down; and there was hardly a sound except the splashing of the oars. Sometimes the bushes crowded up so that there wasn't much room to spare for working them.

Now and then a frog would "kerchunk" into the

stream, as he saw us coming; and sometimes a mud-turtle would slide in. Once I saw a whole family of them sunning on a log, just ahead, and told Joe, who poised his oar to give the end of the log a shove, but they scrambled in all together, like a shot, just before he hit it.

"This is a regular wilderness!" he said; "I wonder how long it'll be before we get through it. I'm going to time it."

So he looked, and found it was quarter past seven. Then he pulled away again; and the trees grew thinner on the east, and let the sun through pretty hot. It was quite swampy here,—bog-tussocks in all directions, with the water glistening among them.

"It's a deal more comfortable in the boat than it would be footing it along here," I remarked.

"Specially if you ain't rowing!"

"Well, I'll take hold awhile—when we get out of the wilderness—so put in, Joe!"

We could see through the trees that the land was getting higher ahead; but just then the stream made a sharp bend to the right, and soon we were in thicker woods than ever. We couldn't see very far in any direction, for the course kept bending.

Suddenly there was a soft scrape underneath, and we came to a stop, with the forward part lifted a little. We looked over, and saw we had run on a log that stretched across underneath the water. It was so dark-colored we could hardly make it out.

JOE WENT OVERBOARD WITH A SLUMP.

"Shove her over, Joe!" and I got up to help while he went forward to get a better "purchase;" then she tilted, with the bow down and stern up; I came down on my hands, and Joe went overboard with a slump!

But quick as a flash he came up and caught the gunwale with one hand, and with the other drew forth his Waterbury, and laid it on the thwart. Then I laughed.

"Come, Joe! a *Water*bury oughtn't to mind a ducking!"

"It doesn't!" he returned, "not half as much as you would, if you'd gone in! Put it in my bag, will you? Blame this log! she's balanced on it; it's a regular see-saw!"

"You take the painter, now you're over, and pull while I shove," said I,

"It's muddy!" he replied; "I'll go ashore and pull."

So he scrambled up the bank, and I threw him the painter, and we got her off in a jiffy. Then we waited a little for him to drip, before he got aboard.

"The *Triton's* getting new tricks!" he said, "bucking and throwing her passengers!"

"O well, she isn't responsible, here in fresh water!" said I. "She isn't used to it."

"I wonder if the salt's soaked out of her planks, yet!"

"It's in a fair way to get soaked out of your shirt! Isn't that the same one you had on when you dropped from the *Medora's* bobstay last Thursday?"

"Same one!" he said; "and the salt's there yet!" he added, chewing the faded blue flannel sleeve. "It'll take more than one douse in this mud-turtle creek to soak that old Mattaconsett brine out!"

He got aboard, and sat down astern, while I took the oars.

CHAPTER XIII.

Not long after, the woods stopped at a fence that came down into the water on each side; there was just room to squeeze through. A little way ahead was a bridge; and this side of it were two cows standing in the water; they jumped, I tell you, when they saw us come splashing out of the woods towards them, and galloped off a little way.

Where they had been, the river widened out, and was pretty shallow, hardly two feet deep, and a road came down and ran across here, right through the water. There was quite a current running; but it slackened beyond, where the stream was narrower, and deep again,— and there was the bridge; but it was only three planks wide, with a railing on one side; and a footpath led to it each way, from the road. We had to bow our heads, to get under.

"That's good economy," said Joe; "no need of a carriage-bridge, when you can ride right across the river."

"What time do you make it? We're out of the wilderness now."

Joe took his watch out of the bag, and said, "Three minutes of eight. Not very long, considering we stopped awhile at that log."

He had taken out a napkin, with which he wiped

his hands, then carefully wiped the watch, and opened it.

"Not a drop got in!" he pronounced, with satisfaction.

"I suppose the world would stop turning 'round, if anything happened to that old turnip!" I observed.

Joe paid no regard to this, but put his turnip back in the bag, and then remarked, "I'm wet enough myself, though; and I'd like to haul ashore in some sunny spot, and take a dry."

"All right,"—and not long after we came to a rocky hillside, stretching up on the left. I pulled inshore, and tossed out the grapnel. Joe took off his clothes and spread them around on the warm rocks; and then we took our bags up under the shade of a big oak, and had breakfast. This time we cleaned out everything but a few eggs and the hard-tack, and the canned salmon. The bags weren't so heavy as they had been, by a deal.

"We'll try for fish, in the next pond we come to," I said. "Let's depend on ourselves, as far as we can."

There were some patches of huckleberries further up, and we picked for half an hour or so, while the clothes were drying, and nearly filled Joe's pail.

Then he dressed; and our exploring expedition again moved up the river. The huckleberry patches grew thicker as we went on, and came down close to the water; presently we saw two sun-bonnets bobbing about among the bushes, a blue and a white one.

When we came up, we found there was a woman, a girl about twelve years old, and two little boys; all busily picking away. Joe asked the old question, "How far to Shad Factory,"—and this time it was about a mile.

"By the road, that is; but I guess *you'll* find it a good deal further. Do you know anybody up there?"

"No; just going up for the fun of it."

"Where're you from?"

"Pierhaven."

"Land sakes!" and she looked as if she thought we were runaways.

I thought it was time for a question on our side; so I asked how many berries they'd got; and she said, "Pretty near a bushel now; we've been picking since daylight. When'd you start from there?"

"Yesterday morning!" I called back, for Joe had set the oars to going again.

In a moment or two, the woman went on picking; but the young ones watched till we were out of sight.

Now the river flowed along a ledge for several rods, where, in some places, the rocks rose bare right from the water, as it did at the island down below. After getting by that, we turned past a low clump of willows, and then the water spread out among several big rocks and gravelly islands, with four or five channels winding between them.

We tried the widest; and after a little while, the gravel came up close to the top; so we backed out, and tried a deep one between two rocks, where most of the water seemed to come through; for there was a swift current.

Joe pulled slowly in against it, I sculling to help him; soon we had to make a turn, where the stream rounded the smaller rock, and then we found the way so narrow that we never could have got by without turning the boat edgewise; so we bumped and scratched back out of that.

"This is getting pretty tough!" I said.

"Yes!— but there's one place left."

But when we came to look at that, we found it was altogether too narrow and crooked; so we made up our minds to lighten her and try to work her over the first place.

We pushed to where it shoaled, and ran her bow up on the gravel. Then we took off shoes and stockings, and got out; that lightened her enough so we could haul her over; we did'nt have to go more than twice her length, before we could float ourselves again.

Then pretty soon we found a place where the main current struck in, and gave us plenty of depth; but it was rather ticklish work still, with stones sticking up here and there, and the current twisting about and slewing her bow this way and that. Though we kept a good look-out for sunken rocks, we just missed running square on one nice jagged specimen, and had to back out once more.

"I wish I'd timed that!" exclaimed Joe, when we at last got through. "I would, if I'd known we were going to have such a tussle!"

"Well, we haven't got to the head of navigation yet, Joe!"

"It wouldn't take many more such places, though, to make me think we were getting pretty near it!"

We brought up to the bank, to rest a few moments after our tugging and shoving. Here it was quite deep, nearly the length of the oar; and about once and a half the boat's length across; so the water had plenty of room, and the current was gentle.

I got out my compass, and took the direction of the next reach; it was just northwest by north. It stretched along for perhaps thirty yards; the land sloping down each way, with woods on the left, and scattered trees, among rocks, on the other side. Then it turned to the right, and we could see nothing further. That was just the beauty of this kind of exploring; you couldn't tell anything about what you might see the next minute.

At last Joe took up the oars again, and when he had rowed a few strokes, we came to a branch opening out from the right, about large enough to crowd the boat into. We saw it wasn't an "affluent," for the water ran into it out of the main stream, and we concluded it must have been split off by the tangle of rocks below, and wandered farther away than the other channels before returning to the river again.

Then the way opened north, nearly straight, for quite a distance; on the left, the bank sloped steeply down from the level field above. Where the river turned again, we could see a house among the trees.

A little way ahead, a fence ran down to the bank, and then along its edge, and as we drew nearer, we saw that opposite the house was another of those little ferry-boat arrangements, with a place dug into the bank for a harbor for the boat, and stone steps leading down from the gate, while on the other side, a path led off across the fields.

A little white-headed chap was hanging to the fence palings, looking through at us.

"Hullo, bub!" hailed Joe.

"Hul-lo!" he said.

Then a little terrier ran down and put his nose through the fence, and yapped. As we passed along, he'd run along, too, a few feet; then put his nose out, and sauce us again. He wanted terribly to get through and devour us, but couldn't.

Joe dipped his hand in and splashed some water up at him, and it put him in such a fury, it seemed as though he'd bark himself inside-out. He had to stop at the fence corner, and then he danced around, while the little chap came up there. too, and looked after us. We heard the dog keeping it up for a minute or two after we'd gone around the bend out of sight.

We saw no one else, but it was rather pleasant to pass so near a house, after so much wilderness, even if we were saluted by nothing more than a baby and a puppy.

Now came a shady reach through some willows, followed by a grove of tall hickories, many of which stood at the water's edge, with the big, gnarled roots washed bare. Then we came on a little bridge, with a fellow leaning on the rail, fishing.

He was a chubby chap about ten years old, and didn't look as if he cared much whether he caught anything or not. But when he saw us coming, he sung out, "Hold on there! you'll scare the fish!"

"That's cool!" muttered Joe. Then he called out, "We'll scare them up to you, more likely. Are there any there?"

"I've caught two."

"Lets land here, and see," I suggested; "if they're worth trying for, we can join in."

So we jumped ashore, and walked up to the bridge.

"Where are your fish?" says Joe.

He looked at us a moment, then seemed to think he'd risk trusting us; for he went one side in the bushes, and got a twig with two little round, flattish fish strung on it, shaped much like a young "scup" (or "porgy," as they call them New York way.) But they were "colored up" considerably more,— a greenish olive, speckled with reddish spots; and there was a sort of an eye-spot on the edge of each gill-cover; black, with a red border part way around.

"They're bream!" said Joe.

"They're punkin'-seed!" corrected the boy,—and they *were* about that shape.

"So now we know what punkin'-seed are!" said I.

"Can't you catch anything else around here?"

'There's bull-points in Harlow's pond, above here,—and they get pickerel there, too, sometimes."

"Well, we're going there, sonny," said Joe, "and I guess you'll find this sort of fish won't scare worth a cent. We'll send you down all we come across."

"Where be you from?" he then asked.

"Pierhaven."

"Come all the way from there in that boat?"

"We did, sonny."

This seemed to impress him so much, that he said nothing more against our passing, but came down and looked at the *Triton* and her belongings, as we got aboard.

When we came to the bridge, we found it so low that it was rather awkward to get under; but by crouching and pushing we managed it, and moved off up-stream; leaving the fisherman to catch his punkin'-seed undisturbed.

CHAPTER XIV.

Not long after, we came to a split in the stream; but the branch was much smaller than the main body of water, and we were not sure about it's being an island. It turned out to be one, though; we reached the end of it in a minute or two; and there were two smaller ones just beyond it,— pretty little islands, with willows on them; and between the willows we could see the water gliding by on the other side. Then the banks rose again, till they were as hig has our heads on each side; and there was a little rivulet rippling down into the river.

"No island this time!" said I, "*that* comes from some spring."

We drew up to it, and I filled the cup; it tasted rather better than the river water,—which we didn't fancy much, though we had been drinking it now and then all day;— still it was rather warm, and not exactly what we wanted.

"If I thought the spring wasn't very far, I'd take the jug up and fill it," said Joe.

"But as he pulled ahead, I suppose he had his doubts about the matter. Presently he pulled out his watch — which was once more in its usual pocket — and said, "Ten minutes to twelve! I thought I was feeling empty."

WE BROUGHT THE BOAT INTO THE COVE.

"Very well, Joe," said I; "I'll take up the oars till twelve, if you like, and then we'll fill up."

But before the ten minutes were up we came on a halting-place which we agreed wasn't likely to be beat,—within the next quarter of a mile, anyway.

The river widened out a little, and made a short, straight reach of may be ten boat-lengths. About midway was a little cove four or five feet deep, with a bright, sandy bottom; and almost opposite was a great beech tree rooted on the edge of the bank, which for some reason had fallen across so that its branches rested on the other bank and propped it up; and it made a kind of arch over the water, as much as ten feet high in the middle.

The tree was growing as bravely as ever, and was thick with leaves, waving up above us and trailing in the water from the lower boughs. The trunk was of such a size that neither of us could reach around it, though the two of us could, easily enough; and the bark was light and smooth, as is always the way with beech trees;—just the thing for cutting your name, and somebody *had* dug in some letters,—before it fell over, I guess; for they were so cracked and bulged we found it hard to make them out;—E. L. H., we thought they looked like.

Well, we brought the boat into the cove, and sat down on a little plat of grass in the shade of the beech, where we ate some crackers and huckleberries and the last of our eggs.

Then we climbed up into the tree, and found lots of little three-cornered beech-nuts, which weren't fit to eat, of course; we wished it could be a couple of months later, just for a few minutes. We got out our knives and cut our initials on the smooth side of one of the big boughs, and under them I put the date.

When we came down I proposed going over to find that spring and fill the jug.

Joe said we ought to be getting on to Harlow's pond, and catch some fish before night; but we finally agreed to start out, and if we didn't reach it in fifteen minutes, to give up and come back.

So I took my pocket folding cup out of the bag,— one of the kind that shuts up like a telescope,— and we went back along the bank till we found the streamlet, and then followed it up. It led us across a field, and under a fence, (but we went over,) then it spread out in a kind of swampy place, all covered with sweet-flag. We pulled up some, and nibbled at the roots; but I don't fancy it much, it's so bitter and burning.

Well, we didn't know but that was the last of our spring; but soon we picked up the stream again beyond, and followed it under another fence into a patch of woods.

"Eight minutes," said Joe, as we entered the woods; so on we hurried, and in less than another minute we came suddenly on it.

The water bubbled out among mossy stones into a little basin, shaded by feathery ferns and tall brakes, and a perfect tangle of wild shrubbery and vines; two slender birches rose from the brink. Nothing could look prettier and more refreshing on a hot July day.

THE SPRING.

Each of us took a good drink, and it was first-rate, and cool as could be. We were afraid of roiling it, if we tried to put the big jug under, so we filled it from the cup, and got back within the half-hour.

It made us hot, hurrying back with that heavy jug; and this time when Joe proposed a bath I was quite willing to join. The little shady cove was a capital place for a dip; and we swam out and caught hold of the beech twigs, and let the cool current slide by us.

When we went back to the cove, to dress, Joe who was ahead, exclaimed, "Hold on — keep still a minute!" and he began to reach cautiously forward for something at the edge of the water, on the farther side. I caught a glimpse of it and scrambled into the boat as quickly as I could get there.

"Joe, let it alone!" I yelled, so loud he was startled, and held back a moment.

"Come away! don't touch it; it's a scorpion! it'll kill you!"

Then he laughed, jabbed out his hand, and picked it up. I was horrified, and expected to hear him yell every instant; and what I could do for him, I didn't know.

"Didn't you ever see a crawfish before?" and he came up to show the wriggling object.

"Don't hold it over the boat! Crawfish? I've seen the word often; but I thought it *was* a fish, and not such a looking beast! It's more like the picture of a scorpion than anything else I ever saw!"

And it was. It had two big claws,— big for its size,— and a long tail; altogether it was nearly as long as my hand.

"It can't hurt you, any more than a fiddler-crab. Its a kind of little fresh-water lobster, don't you see?"

I saw that it didn't seem to hurt *him* any; but I didn't like the looks of the creature, and felt better when Joe flung him off into the stream.

I suppose the boys who are used to big streams and ponds of fresh water, will think I was a precious ignoramus; but this was the only piece of running water in our region that you couldn't jump across; and what ponds there were were to match. I had been to Boston and New York, but never back from the coast any distance; and if any fresh-water-fellows, such as don't know a clam from a quahaug, should come my way, I reckon I could tangle them up some; for I'll engage to show ten salt-water creatures for every fresh-water one they can bring on.

When we were dressed, I took the oars, and on we went again. We turned to the eastward; and for a little while the way led through a rather swampy region, of no particular interest; but after we had rounded about a dozen bends, there was one of the prettiest sights I'd ever seen.

The river was thickly fringed with young, slender trees, on each side; hardly any bigger than your wrist; and they arched over and ran into each other above our heads, with leaves so thick we could hardly see a bit of sky; still there were plenty of places where the sun struck through, so that the place was full of warm, shimmering light.

This stretched straight in front of us for a good ways; there was a little wind outside, for the leaves shook and quivered a trifle here and there; but the water was perfectly still, except where the little eddies were curling and spreading; and you could hardly tell where it began, and the air left off.

It was a grotto or tunnel, of all shades of bright and dark green; with the dark trunks and twigs stretching up over and branching around; and then another set started down from them and branched out underneath—the reflections, you know—and these were waving and running together, first in one place, then another.

Joe stopped rowing, and I sculled gently a few moments, just enough to hold her against the current, while we looked at it. It seemed a pity to set to and row, and go splashing through it, but of course we did.

But when we turned the corner, there was just such another reach, only not as long. Then the trees grew larger, and the underbrush was shorter and more scraggly; so it wasn't as interesting.

Later on, though, we came to another lovely tunnel, which would have been as handsome as the first if we could have seen as much of it at a time; but it kept curving around, so it was hard to tell how long it really was.

" I wonder if anybody's seen these places before?" said I.

"Of course some one must have, some time or other in this settled region!"

"Well, perhaps so, but not very often, I guess. I doubt whether it ever comes into people's heads around here that there's anything to be seen. It's a matter of course to them, they've always known it; that is, they see it where the roads and bridges go across, and where it bounds the pastures, and never think of there being anything more to it."

"But we know there's where they're mistaken!" remarked Joe.

"Indians may have come paddling down through here, sometimes," I went on, "but not often, I should think. They wouldn't find any use in it; the things they hunted were on land, and they could scour across the country in less than half the time it takes to follow, round these bends."

CHAPTER XV.

After this reach ended, a point of rocks ran into the stream, forcing it off to the left, where it ran quite swiftly through a narrow channel.

Beyond, the land sloped down steeply to the water, with willows fringing along the shore, coming out brightly against the dark oaks behind, on the slope. Some of these oaks were tall, grand-looking trees.

"We've been shut in for more than an hour, with never a glimpse outside!" declared Joe. "We've been exploring the river, I know; but I'd like to see something more of the country we've been through!"

So we fastened the boat, and walked up the hill to a place where we could look between the trees over the way we had come. We couldn't see the river at all. We thought we could make out where it flowed under the trees in some places — where they were in long, curving lines like a great hedge; but there was no making sure.

We weren't very high up, though; and I don't believe we could see more than a mile in any direction; and behind us the trees rose thickly.

"It's plain enough that the only way to see this river along here, is to sail on it, the way we're doing," said Joe.

"And I shouldn't wonder if we're the only ones who have seen it for some time back. We've seen only one boat besides our own, since we started, that's fit to explore in."

We found the banks steep for some distance further, sometimes rocky, with junipers and birches, sometimes thickly wooded with oaks or hickories; while now and then a willow would trail the tips of its switches in the stream.

When we came to flat country again, we wound through a grove of oaks; the trees standing well apart, without underbrush; and a drove of hogs were rooting about. Those nearest came close up and grunted inquiringly from the bank; and we replied with some choice imitations of pig's music; but I doubt whether we said anything they understood.

After leaving the grove, the river spread out to twice its ordinary width, and the current was very gentle; so we made good progress. We could see the bottom plainly; it wasn't more than a yard deep.

Soon we saw a rock standing out alone in the middle, with a flat top about a foot above water. Two logs met on the rock, one leading from each shore; we didn't expect to find a bridge with a double span so far up.

There was hardly more than room enough for the boat to scrape under; so we got out on the rock, then reached down, and shoved her along through.

Now an old worm-fence came down, so matted and tangled with vines it could scarcely be seen; and beyond it the river narrowed again. Soon there was a perfect jungle of bushes and small trees on either side; they didn't arch over gracefully, but stuck out all ways, tangled here and open there; and we had to poke them out of the way, where they stretched across and dipped in.

The stems crowded into the water so it was hard to keep the oars out of them; and when we had come to a dead stop twice, by getting caught in sharp turns, Joe thought he would try rowing on one side. So he drew in his starboard oar, and took both hands to the other one, while I pointed her a little way from the middle.

There was room enough now, most of the time; but we weren't satisfied, by any means; for the water ran swifter through here than at any place yet; and though I helped by sculling as much as I could, I had to take care to offset his one-sided work; and we crawled along at less than a mile an hour.

So we tried another way. We both stood up; I faced sternways and thrust at the tree-stems, while Joe, in the bow, faced forwards, and paddled first on one side, then on the other; and when we came to a bend, he'd jab sideways against the trees, and force her bow around.

He had to attend to the steering, now. When he sung out "Steady!" I knew there was a straight

stretch ahead, and put in and shoved for all I was worth. When we came to a bend, he'd call "port!" or "Starboard" according as it turned; and we'd fetch her around as well as we could. When the bend was sharp we had to turn her as though she was pivoted amidships. When he yelled "branch!" I knew it was stoop or be raked;—and he had to keep that racket up most of the time. My hat was scraped off the first thing, and we lost ten yards before I got it again; I didn't put it on, but stowed it in the boat.

This was pretty hard work, but it was fun, too; and we certainly went a deal faster. Anybody'd have laughed to have seen us — the boat swaying and pitching along, the twigs crackling and scratching, and we digging and thrusting every way like mad; the oars slipping now and then, and nearly letting us overboard. But it wasn't a kind of work that you could take easy, and be graceful about; it had to be done that way or not at all.

Well, we staved along, till I, at least, was nearly blown; I hadn't had much idea of our direction for the last ten minutes, and we didn't seem to be getting anywhere.

"Hold on!" I panted; "let's tie up and rest a minute!"

We were at a bend, and Joe said, "It's better ahead; give her another shove or two!"

So we brought her into the next stretch, and tied

up to a limb. It *was* a little better; wider and larger trees. But as soon as we stopped splashing we found the air was full of a low, rushing sound.

"A waterfall!" said I. "Or rapids, may be," suggested Joe.

There was something of the sort, no doubt; for here and there little foam spots came floating past us. But nothing could be seen beyond the leafy walls of the short reach we were in.

Of course it wasn't a minute before we were ready to go ahead again. We rounded the bend, and the noise was a deal louder,—close by,—but the boughs stretching across in front were so dense we couldn't see.

We could see the water, though; and there was something there besides the reflection of leaves and sky,—there was the broken wavering image of a gray stone wall, pierced with black windows! We pushed out under the willows,—and ten yards in front, the river was lost to sight, where it flowed from the dark arch of a mill raceway!

CHAPTER XVI.

Above and beyond the raceway, rose the mill. There could be no doubt that this was the "Shad Factory" towards which we had been working by such a winding course.

It was a small affair for a cotton factory; stone-built, on the further side of a road which led across the raceway, and up the hill to the east. The trees grew thick and tall, from where we were clear up to the road.

Most of the windows were thrown open, and the clatter, clack and buzz, poured out among the tree-tops; it was this we had heard, rather than the rush of water, which was falling over the dam in only two or three slender streams, uniting in the middle of a broad channel which led down under the road, and emptied into the river close beside the arch before us.

"Shad Factory is ours!" cried Joe. "Let us note the proud moment — 3:17 P.M. on Tuesday, July 23d, after unexampled struggles and catastrophes, this heroic pair beheld the goal of their indomitable efforts!"

"But even then their zeal knew no pause!" I continued.

"Not a bit!" assented Joe. "But if we follow

up much farther on this line, we'll get chawed up, sure! Our galleon 'll have to traverse the dusty earth for a spell. We'd better scare up some of the natives, to lend us a hand and get her around the dam!"

We could see some of the operatives through the windows, busily working; but they hadn't caught sight of us. After working the boat up against the swift, foam-speckled current, we walked up the bank on our left, towards the road.

We now saw a cluster of small tenement-houses, the homes of the operatives. A woman was taking some clothes off a line, and near her a few hens were scratching about; a little girl was perched in a swing, with two or three smaller infants frisking around; and a big yellow dog, chained to a tree, was so fast asleep that our steps didn't rouse him.

The only creature who seemed to see us, was a dirty-white goat, who stood stock-still, and kept his eyes steadily on us.

We didn't stop to interview any of these people, for we had caught sight of a few boys fishing on the edge of the pond, near the dam, and that was more like what we wanted. We started for them; and they saw us, too, and looked us over while we were coming up.

I hardly know which party passed the most creditable inspection; we weren't wearing our best clothes; and if we had been, they'd have gone through enough in these two days to take the freshness off. Whatever they thought of us, they seemed a rather seedy-looking set.

Two of them we put down as "Frenchies," or French Canadians, such as were common among the factory workers at home; the other three were plainly country boys of the neighborhood. These last were about our age; the "Frenchies," a little older.

They had among them nine fish; six were rather ugly, big-headed fellows, six or eight inches long, black above and light-colored below, and without scales, like an eel; they had some short feelers around their lips, and queer little sullen-looking black eyes, with white rims. These were "bull-pouts," or cat-fish.

The rest were handsome greenish-gold fishes, with half-a-dozen dark bands across the back, and half-way down the sides; and the lower or "ventral" fins, were orange-colored. Joe told me afterward that they were perch.

He spoke first: "How long have you been fishing?"

"'Bout two hours," answered one of the country fellows.

"Not biting very lively to-day, then?"

For a moment nothing was said, then one ventured, "You're from up the road, ain't you?"

"No."

"O, you've come from down Woodword way, then?"

"Not that either!" said Joe, with a smile.

"Well, which way *did* ye come, then?"

"Up the river."

One of the "Frenchies" said something I couldn't hear, and another boy said, "Oh, they're from the brick-yard, Bill!"

"Not a bit! we're from Pierhaven!"

We didn't quite fancy being taken for brick-yard boys.

"Gracious! d'you come all that to-day? Got your boat here?" he went on.

"Yes; and there's a chance for you fellows to earn a quarter, by helping us to bring her up here to the pond."

When they heard that they thought a deal more of us, and they dropped their poles and came right along.

"Ho! she's flat-bottomed!" said Bill, "we can haul her right over!"

"You can haul her on the grass, but we must lift her the rest of the way; I don't want to scrape the bottom off her!"

So we took out most of the things; the two "Frenchies" seized hold of the painter, while the rest of us took hold along the sides, and we "snaked" her up the bank and across the grass to the road, in a jiffy.

We stuck to it that she must be lifted the rest of the way, so the biggest fellow took hold at the bow and walked backwards, two at each side staggered along sideways, and two had hold at the stern. We had to put her down once, and rest a moment; not that she was so very heavy, but she was awkward to pick up and walk with; there were no places convenient to take hold of. We said we'd rig some handles on her before we tried much more of this sort of work.

The dog had roused up, and was "giving tongue" with all his might; but he'd traveled around the tree and wound himself up so tight he could hardly stretch out enough to bark; his collar choked him so that every moment or two he had to stop and cough before he could go on. I've read plenty of stories about smart dogs, but I never saw or heard of one that was smart enough to unwind his chain from such a fix.

The young ones had run up and were trotting around us; there were nigh a dozen now; the woman at the clothes-line had stopped to look; there were several heads at the windows, and an old chap in overalls, with a pipe, stood in one of the doors; some people were looking out now from the factory, and one yelled something at us, we couldn't hear what; and the dog kept cheering us on! But the goat stuck where he was, and just kept his head pointed our way; and the hens paid no attention at all.

So, after her long passage through the wilderness, the *Triton* was at last lugged across amid this uproar and parade, and launched safely in the pond.

Joe paid the quarter like a man; but they weren't equal to dividing it around; so he took it back, and found a dime for the "Frenchies," and a dime and nickel for the others.

Then the country chaps had to fire off a lot of questions, which seemed likely to end in Joe's telling all about how we camped out, and what we'd been through. Meanwhile those hens had put a thought in my head; and I asked one of the "Frenchies" if he'd any eggs to sell. He started off at the word; and in a minute he was back with twenty-one in a tin pan; but I didn't want to take more than a dozen, for I didn't know how long they'd been laid;— for the dozen he wanted to charge us twenty cents:

"Bother!" says Joe, "leave 'em alone; we can get 'em for half that at the next farm-house!" and he began to cast off the painter.

Then the fellow offered the lot for Joe's quarter; and we agreed to it if he'd throw in some bait. So Joe handed over, and we bagged the eggs; and they gave us an old tin box half-full of earth-worms; and then I hurried Joe off; for I saw three or four men starting from the factory, and the old chap with the pipe had put on his hat, and was half-way to us—and I thought there was no reason why we should stand and be catechised the rest of the afternoon.

We had barely shoved off, before the crowd offered us their fish for another quarter; but we didn't see it. "Ten cents!" they yelled; but we had finished trading for that time.

"That set don't see silver every day!" remarked Joe.

We'd forgotten to ask where the best fishing was, so we concluded to experiment about a little. It wasn't a very wide pond,—the dam and the factory pretty nearly measured it, that way; but it stretched up northwestwardly for quite a distance, and then bent around to the north; so that we weren't sure that we saw the end of it.

I took the oars; and it was a comfort to row once more where there was plenty of room, and I could pull around any way, without running ashore in three strokes; it hadn't been so since we left Wylie's bridge, the morning before.

There was a little sail-boat tied up to the bank, and two other boats were in sight along the shore; but no one seemed to be out fishing.

"Think of any one's keeping a sail-boat on this little pond!" I exclaimed.

"Yes; if 'twas Lake Superior, 'twould be different."

"Rather, I should say! How queer it must seem to be out of sight of land on *fresh* water; to have big waves send fresh-water spray over you! and, more than all, to see fresh-water surf pounding on the beach! It seems as if I could hardly believe it, even if I saw it; I can imagine volcanoes and cyclones, easier!"

I pulled till we judged we were a little past the middle of the pond; and then we hove over the grapnel; it struck at about fifteen feet. Then we got out our hand-lines, baited them and threw them over, salt-water fashion. We thought we felt a few nibbles; but they were precious feeble ones.

"Come!" said Joe, "this is no use; we must do as the Romans do, and get some poles."

There were some birches on the shore right opposite; and we "up keleg,"— I mean, we pulled up the anchor,— and started for them. It didn't take long to hack down and trim a couple of poles,— they weren't beauties, but we judged the bullpouts hadn't style enough themselves, to mind.

Then we had to put on floats, or "dobbers"; we tossed for the cork of the jug, and Joe got it. He said fresh-water fish didn't hang round the bottom, but swam a little way from the top; so he tied his dobber on about four feet from the hooks; but my idea was that they'd go for something to eat, wherever they saw it, if there wasn't anything to frighten them away; and the farther the hook was from us, the less they'd see to be scared at.

He said that sounded well enough; but his was the way they always did. There'd be no harm in trying both ways, I thought; so I hunted a little and found a bit of soft pine on the shore, which I tied on about ten feet from the hooks.

We got the boat anchored again, a little nearer the shore, and Joe was the first to throw over,— slup! it went to the bottom, dragging the cork down after it.

"I thought your fish lived in the upper story!" said I.

"Confound it! I forgot to take off that big lead sinker!"

So he pulled in again, and got it off; but he said there must be something to carry the hooks down, so he rumaged out some boat-nails we kept in the locker, and fastened on one; and I rigged one on mine the same way.

Then we flung our lines out; it's safe to believe there wasn't much "science" about our "casting," but we managed to keep clear of each other. Then the proper thing was to watch our "dobbers"; but it wasn't very exciting business. I'd thrown over on the sunny side, to be out of Joe's way; but there was such a glare on the water that I drew in and made another cast over the bow; and then we settled down and waited.

CHAPTER XVII

It was comfortable and lazy; but it grew dull pretty soon; and Joe said he was going to throw out some "ground-bait." So he took about half our worms, cut them into bits and sprinkled 'em overboard; they sunk slowly, and we watched them as long as we could see; but nothing seemed to come for them. When we fished down at Pierhaven, if we threw over as much as a clam-shell, we could see the "chogsetts" squabbling over it and jerking it around before it had sunk a fathom.

But the "ground-bait" seemed to do the business, for in two or three minutes Joe said something was at his line. His float was wiggling and dancing a little, and in a moment it went almost under. Then he gave a jerk, and out came the fish which swung wriggling into the boat. It was a bull-pout.

"Now see here!" said Joe, "you can't grab this fellow, anyhow. See this sharp spine in front of his back fin, and these two on each side, sticking straight out?"

"Yes; the first ray of the pectoral fins."

"Just so; well, he'd like nothing better than to get those horns into your hand; that's why they call these fish horn-pouts, sometimes. Now I take hold of the line close to his mouth, so he can't flop around, and then take him with the other hand, two fingers on each side, right behind the horns, and then I've got him so he can't do any harm."

He found it rather troublesome to get the hook out, after all; for the greedy little rascal had swallowed it more than half-way through him, like a "toad-grunter." Then I saw my float joggle, and pulled up, but there was nothing. It stayed still after that, while Joe brought in two more; so I concluded the fish must be nearer the top that day, and tied my float lower down. Then it wasn't long before I got one bigger than any of Joe's.

"Bull-pout, horn-pout, bull-head, catfish," said I. "'Tisn't every little homely fish can sport such a string of names!"

"And of course he's got a Latin name, too, as long as all of 'em together,—if we only knew what it was!" added Joe.

"But they're not all so little, either. There are catfish in the Mississippi River as big as a man, and they catch them with such tackle as we use for sharks."

"Yes, I've heard fish stories before!"

"No; it's so, honest. I've seen a picture of men catching such a one, with big gaff-hooks to land him with."

"Well, they must be diabolical-looking beasts! I'd rather have a shark at the end of my line!"

Then I hauled in another—not a shark, but a little catfish hardly longer than my finger; a sort of *kitten*-fish, but, unlike kittens, he was just as ugly as the old ones. Just after, Joe got another. This fresh-water fishing wasn't so bad for a change.

"Talking about names," remarked Joe, "most fish seem to be well off that way. There's bream, and pumpkin-seed; and the salt-water fishes, too,—what we call 'scup,' are 'porgies,' down in Long Island Sound."

"I know it; and 'tautog' are called 'blackfish,' down there. And 'chogsetts,'—they're 'cunners,' Down East—but Captain Sayre says the true name's 'blue perch.'"

"Rock perch,' I've heard 'em called; but 'burgall' is the old original name, so uncle says."

"Well! there's another string of names for a little six-inch fish! And the minnows, that we call 'nippers' and 'mummychogs,' Fred Scovill's cousin from Poughkeepsie called 'killie-fish,' when he was on here last summer, because they lived in the creeks or kills;—that's what the old Dutch settlers called them—Kaatskill, Peekskill, you know."

"Yes," said Joe, "and there's 'squiteague,' that we catch in the bay now and then, and think we've got something uncommon; they haul those in by the boat-load, below New York Bay; and there they're 'weak-fish.'"

"'Weak-fish!' I have heard of them; but I didn't know they meant 'squiteague!'"

"And 'quahaugs' they call 'hard clams,'"—but here he had to attend to another bull-pout who had established communication. When it had joined the others above water, he went on:

"You see we've kept up the old Indian names more than they have in other places; perhaps their ears weren't cultivated up to the beauties of the native lingo."

Then I pulled in another fish, a perch this time, and pretty enough to make up for the unsightliness of the bull-pouts.

Somebody else was now fishing not far away. He had a blue coat, and white waistcoat, with a blue sash across it, and wore a big blue fuzzy cap; he was sitting on the limb of an old dead tree by the shore, and didn't have any pole.

All at once he took a header right in, with his spruce suit all on! but he was out in a second, and had a fish — in his mouth.

'Twas a kingfisher; and he gulped his catch in a moment, and set himself for another. We saw him dive twice; and he got one each time. They weren't very big; still, I don't see where he stowed 'em all. Perhaps then he thought he had enough; for all of a sudden he streaked off, leaving his usual farewell song singing behind him, about as melodious as a watchman's rattle.

They weren't biting as well now; but I caught another perch, while Joe had nothing but bull-pout.

At last, however, he hooked a little fellow different from any we had taken. His shape was midway between the bream and perch ; but his back fin was smaller, and his tail was notched so deeply as almost to divide it in two. He was'nt marked like them, but was a light bronze all over, except his back, which was darker. Joe said he was a "shiner."

It was well towards five o'clock ; and we wanted to get our fish cooked before dark ; so we counted up, and found we had nine bull-pouts, two perch, and a shiner; besides three too small to be of any account. So we said we'd leave after one more throw.

That time, strange to say, each of us caught a bream ! their crowd must have just heard of the free lunch.

There was a little wind from the north, and we spread the sail. When last used, it had been a tent.

There were low hills around the pond, with several houses in sight, besides the tenement-houses and the factory, the hum of which was borne to us over the water. We glided quite near the little sail-boat, not as large as our own craft, and painted bright red, with a white stripe ; "Ella" showed in white on the stern. She was moored with her bow almost touching the shore.

"There's no tide to go out and leave her stranded," I said.

There were thick woods around the upper part of the pond, chiefly on the north side; and among them we soon made out the place where the stream flowed in. We were now to enter unknown regions, indeed; we had heard of "Shad Factory," but of nothing farther up.

The pond tapered gradually, and at last the woods closed in on either side; we took the sail down,— and in two minutes more the pond was out of sight, and I was pulling around a long bend to the east, with Joe sitting at the steering-oar.

"Seems natural, doesn't it?" said he.

"Yes, it does. I wouldn't have minded if the pond had held out for a mile or two longer."

Still, it wasn't bad at all here; especially when compared with what we had last tackled in up-stream navigation. There was plenty of room for the oars, the current was gentle; and the trees were fair-sized, and didn't seem to want to get into the water.

In fifteen or twenty minutes we passed the woods, and wound around through some rather swampy pasture-land, with plenty of cattle-tracks stamped around in the soft places, but no beast in sight. Then the land grew higher, and we swept into a bright green meadow, whose turf was cropped short by sheep, a few of which could be seen some distance ahead, where the ground sloped up to a long, low ledge of rocks.

We both thought this might be a good place to camp.

"We'll build a fire-place to cook our fish, somewhere up among those rocks," said Joe.

We rounded a big bend, where the water notched in and made a cove, covered with tall flags, over which the dragon-flies were poising and skimming, and brought up at a level green bank, opposite the nearer end of the ledge.

The kettle was needed to carry up the fish; so we emptied what huckleberries were left upon some leaves which we plucked from an oak close by, and laid upon the grass under it. Then we loaded them into the kettle, and made our way up to the ledge.

In a sort of corner of the rock, where it rose straight from the ground, we laid a large flat stone, and piled other stones on each other at each side; so that at last we had a fire-place, and a bit of chimney above. There wasn't much wood around, but we went off some distance to where the trees were thicker, and in five minutes we'd piled together as many dead branches as we could drag.

When we got back, Joe started the fire, while I went down to the boat for the hatchet; then I set to work to break up our wood. Joe carried the fish to a flat place on the rock, and began to get them in shape for cooking.

He made a good deal of fuss about it, and said they were the worst things he had ever tackled;— slimy as eels, some of the spines sticking straight out, others stiffened half-way up. Finally he went to the boat, and got a stout two-tined fork he had there, and jabbed it into their heads to hold on by; then he got along easier.

Meanwhile I cut up all the wood, and went and got another lot; for the fire used it up fast. Joe got the fish all skinned; and we wished we could cook 'em in as short a time, for we were pretty hungry; but we knew it wouldn't be hot enough for half an hour;—and an hour would likely be better, if we could wait so long.

CHAPTER XVIII.

We heaped some wood on the fire, and we went to get our tents ready; that would take up part of the time. When I opened my bag, to get out the mosquito-netting and pins, there were the eggs; we had forgotten all about them.

"Let's cook 'em all!" proposed Joe; "what we can't eat to-night we'll carry; they'll carry safer cooked."

So I washed out the kettle and dipped it full of of water; then we carried it and the bags to the fire. Next, we must rig a crane to hang the kettle on; but the fire was so lively it was altogether too hot for comfort close by it. It went down soon, though, while we were choosing our sticks and trimming them into proper shape,

Of course, on each side of the fire we planted a stick with a fork at the top, and rested another stout one across the forks. We slung the kettle with some copper wire we happened to have aboard, and waited for it to boil.

Joe had brought a frying-pan, but there was nothing to grease it with; for, strange to say, neither of us had thought to bring any butter. Joe said he had it in mind, at the time he put in the pan, but he would have to go to the keg in the cellar for it, so he didn't just then; and that was the end of it, as far as he was concerned.

So our idea was to cover the stones with leaves, and bake the fish; but we weren't sure how it would work. If we had been at the shore at low tide, we would have piled rock-weed on the stones and put in the fish and they'd have cooked splendidly. But now, we must make the best of what we had.

"Let's boil some of the fish, as well as the eggs," I suggested. "What doesn't turn out well one way, may the other."

"All right! we'll have a chowder and a bake!"

When the water boiled, the eggs were dropped in, one by one. Three turned end up, and we said those weren't fresh-laid. Joe got out his watch.

"I'll give 'em ten minutes; eggs need to be solid when they're going on exploring expeditions!"

When they were done, we had a tough time getting them out. The kettle was nearly full of bubbling water, and we could do nothing with our teaspoons. I got the tips of my fingers in, and then I gave up, while the spoon sank down among the eggs.

Then each of us took a couple of sticks a foot long, and exercised our skill in trying to pinch the eggs between them, and lift them out. We got two out, and let them slap on to the stones. Of course we might have taken the kettle off, and poured out the whole business on the grass, but we didn't like to do that, for then we must wait for another lot of water to heat, and we wanted to start the fish along right off.

We did compromise, though, by setting the kettle on the ground where we could get at it easier, and not be cooking ourselves at the fire; then we soon poked the eggs up over the edge, and let them drop safely on the grass, after a quarter of an hour's lively boiling.

"We ought to dye 'em, and save 'em till next Easter!" declared Joe. "They'll stand anything, now!"

The kettle was re-hung, and half the fish put in, with some hard-tack and a little salt. "When they begin to drop apart, I guess they'll be done."

We put on some wood, and went to gather leaves,—oak-leaves, as being tough and less likely to crumble and stick to the fish. More pulpy leaves would have made more steam, which is what really does the cooking in a well-regulated sea-side bake, but we had doubts about the flavor of steam from leaves; we knew it couldn't be the same as from the crisp, salt rock-weed.

I suggested bayberry leaves; and this reminded us to fill our pillows, which we had emptied in the morning. We had to walk a good way before finding any bayberry bushes; at last we came on a large clump, and I plucked an armful of twigs to add to the oak-leaves.

The fire was getting low, but the water was still boiling; the sun was getting low, too; and we made up our minds to wait no longer. The brands were cleared out, and the flat stone was dusted off with twigs, and covered with a double layer of oak-leaves; then the fish were laid on and strewn with sprigs of bayberry, over which we heaped the rest of the oak-leaves.

Joe took his fork and poked at the fish in the kettle, and concluded they were done; but the water was still boiling, and we left them in a while longer, to make sure.

"I'm afraid they'll get charred on the under side, before they're cooked on top!" said I.

"We'll turn them, then."

So after ten minutes we raked away the leaves enough so we could poke them over, then covered them again. It smelled good and like supper; and Joe took off the kettle and poured out most of the water, and we spooned the fish out into our tin plates; the meat split and crumbled off considerably, so we judged it was done.

When it cooled a little we tried it; and it was pretty good, only fresh; but we had plenty of salt to sprinkle over. We ate some of the eggs, too;

and the three light ones, which we'd set off apart we cracked, and found they were too far gone; so we let 'em drive against one of the trees.

We finished up the huckleberries, too; and the hard-tack that was in with the fish; and altogether we made out a first-rate supper without touching the fish we were baking on the stone. We had to drink the river-water, for Joe had kicked over the jug, without noticing, while he was fishing; and as the cork was on his line, of course our spring-water all ran out.

Finally we took our fish out of the "bake," and laid them on a clean stone; they weren't done very evenly! some parts were about black and others rather tough,— still, some was fairly good, only smoky-tasting;— any way, we gathered them all between two tin plates, to save for breakfast.

It was getting pretty dusky now, and we started to carry the things down to the boat. About half-way, Joe stopped short, and said, "Hold on! now face 'round, and look up hill!"

So I 'bout-faced; but didn't see anything out of the way.

"Now look over this way!"— pointing sou'west. So I looked,— and there was the new moon!

"I saw it over my left shoulder," said he, " now you've seen it over your right; so maybe we'll keep a fair average share of luck for the expedition!"

"Now, Joe," said I, "how much stock do you take in that bosh?"

"Well! I don't know as any, really; only it's a kind of a habit. It doesn't make me 'specially desperate, if I happen to see it the wrong way,— but I'd a little *rather* see it over the right."

We put things in the boat, and turned back up the hill again, for we weren't sleepy yet.

"Come, Joe!" said I, "what's the use of paying any attention to that stuff? this is an enlightened age. If I'd known what you were about, I'd have turned the left shoulder on purpose. The lower down you go among savages, the more signs you run across!"

"Well, we're going back to savage life a little, just now!"

"No we're not; explorers are right in the front of progress. Suppose Stanley carried any such moonshine foolishness into Africa?"

"Well, I know of course it does'nt make any difference really; I've taken notice. Now, there's another sign you can see this minute— 'the old moon in the new moon's arms.' I was told that meant bad weather coming, so long ago I don't remember when. I never took the trouble to notice whether it was true."

"Well, there *is* a grain of sense in that. I suppose you know what makes it."

"Yes; the dark part of the moon's lighted from

the earth; it's in moonlight, you may say, and the crescent is the sunlighted part."

"Well if the air is hazy, so as to make a bright glow in the sky after sunset, as there was last night, you're not so likely to see the 'old moon,' because the glow fades it out; though you can still see the moon, plainly enough. But when it's clear as a bell, like this, your sign shows; and such clear weather is 'most always followed by a storm in a day or two."

"I hope that sign won't come true this time, though."

"So do I. There's another true moon-sign,—a ring around the moon means wet weather coming."

"Yes; and they say the number of stars you can see inside the ring shows how many days it will be before the storm comes."

"Well, now, that part of it is sheer nonsense; you can see that yourself. The moon has a motion of its own, and the same stars won't be near it all night. Besides, if you had a good telescope, you could see, may be, fifty or a hundred stars inside."

"That's so," admitted Joe.

The evening star was shining brightly; not very near the moon, but it reminded me of another sign, more ridiculous still, if anything,

Some sailors believe that if a big star is dogging the moon, as they call it, a storm is sure to follow. Sam Bowers was talking about the big gale in

March, last year; and he said he'd been expecting it, for he'd seen one star ahead of the moon, towing her, and another astern, chasing her. "I know'd 'twas coming, safe enough!" he said.

Joe laughed at that; and wondered what he'd have said if he'd noticed it just after the gale, instead of before.

"He'd have laid any storm to it that happened within a month after!"

"I've seen the moon in the daytime."

"So have I, lots of times; it looks like a little bit of cloud. I've seen it close to a big white cloud; and the cloud was the brightest. I've sometimes wished that one of those great piled-up clouds, forty times as big as the full moon, such as you see hot afternoons, could flash out in the sky of a sudden, some dark night, all lighted up as it was in the day time, — wouldn't it be glorious!"

"Yes; and everybody'd think the world was coming to an end!"

We sat on the ledge and talked a little longer, till the evening star dipped out of sight, and the moon began to set in its turn. Then we found it a trifle chilly; and as there was a little wood left, we heaped it into our fire-place, and warmed up.

"We've got a camp-fire, this time!" said Joe.

Then we talked about a name for the camp. Joe said we might call it "Camp Harlow," after the pond; but the pond wasn't in sight from where we were. I proposed, in fun, "Camp Lunatics," because we'd been discussing crazy notions about the moon; but Joe thought that sounded too much like twitting on ourselves; he said "Camp Luna"'d be just the thing, though; for here we'd seen the moon starting out on her month's voyage.

So we made it "Camp Luna," and turned in; Joe had the boat, this time. 'Twas comfortable under the blanket; and I went to sleep right away.

CHAPTER XIX.

Some time in the night I woke up — not really cold, but the blanket seemed rather thin, and I couldn't seem to get asleep again. I wished I had Joe's "turnip," to see what time it was; I twisted over two or three times, trying to get as much blanket around me as I could — then sat up and wriggled into my clothes.

I lifted a corner of the netting and peeped out; a good part of the sky was covered with clouds, and a few stars shone through the rifts, here and there. I could see the bowl of the "dipper," which lay toward the east, tipped part way up, so it would spill about half, so I judged it must be near morning; for it was standing straight up on the west side of its circle, the evening before.

I lay down again, but couldn't feel sleepy. It seemed a week since we had left home; I wondered what would happen to us that day, and whether we would reach the "head of navigation."

The tree-tops opposite began to look blacker against the sky; presently I heard the roosters echoing each other from all around, and our third day of exploration was dawning on us. The river in front began to show up, a silver-gray streak — but the trees and grass were all one. Then there were some dim whitish spots; those were rocks; the tree-trunks near the river came out black, and the trees near by began to show darker than those a good way off.

It was rosy, now, over in the east; and the birds were in grand chorus. Now I could tell where the trees left off, and the grass began.

I saw Joe's tent shake, and presently he made his appearance at the stern of the *Triton*. He didn't see fit to plunge overboard this morning, but hurried into his clothes, took the plates, with the fish, and the hatchet, and went up to the ledge, where he proceeded to start a fire. He glanced my way as he passed; but I was all quiet under the blanket.

I crept out softly, and managed to dodge around to the other side of the rocks, without his noticing me. When I was opposite to him, and only a few feet off, I raised a tremendous yell and scrambled to the top of the ledge.

Joe was looking wild, and had the hatchet

raised; but he lowered it when he saw me and exclaimed, "Great Cæsar! I didn't know there was room in you for such a screech! It lifted me 'most out of my shoes!"

I told him I thought I'd let him see how it seemed to be surprised by the natives, as sometimes happened to explorers; and he said I came pretty near finding how it seemed to be tomahawked, and that happened to them sometimes, too.

"Seems to me you dressed pretty quick!" he added; "you were all tucked in, just now."

"So I was; but all the same I'd had my clothes on for a quarter of an hour, to keep warm."

"Oh, that's it! Why didn't you make up the fire, then? Come along now and get some more wood; that'll warm you up!"

We brought the wood, and we were soon warmed up, including the fish. We thought we'd try to catch a few more before starting up-stream again; we could row down to the pond in fifteen or twenty minutes.

After breakfasting on whatever of the fish was eatable — which included, I dare say, a good many morsels we wouldn't have thought of touching at the home table, — and helping out with some eggs and hard tack, we struck camp, spreading our blankets on the ledge where the sun had a good chance at them. Then we pulled down to the pond, and cast anchor a little way north of where we fished before.

They took more readily to the bait, this time; and we began hauling in bullpout right away. In a little while Joe's float was suddenly jerked clear under; he twitched up, and swung out a fish about a foot long, but slender, and sharp-nosed; he was very lively and savage, and his mouth was cut away back, like an alligator's. This was a pickerel; and the biggest fish we had caught so far.

Joe was in high feather, now;—"high hook," he said he was, and we were both alert for another; but no more came, and the biting slackened off; though we got a few more of the ordinary kinds.

"We'll keep on till 7:30," said Joe; and he pulled out his infallible Waterbury.

"Twenty minutes of nine, already! it can't be, and sun no higher than this!"

"Of course it can't! you'll have to put the brakes on that old machine!"

"It isn't going!" he now said, with some consternation.

"Well, I'm sure that's nothing to wonder at. You expect altogether too much, I tell you! I suppose she's warranted to go when she's carried! Shake her up!"

"Shut your head! 'tisn't that; it's all right

enough, only I forgot to wind it up, last night! Never mind; I'll set it at seven by guess, and we'll get the time at the first house we come across."

"I'll show you something better than that," said I; "here's something that doesn't need winding up!"

I opened my bag, and took out a flat box, about as large as the palm of my hand, which I opened; and there was an oval dial-plate with the hours of the day marked around, from four in the morning to eight in the evening, and with half and a quarter-hour divisions; one-third of these last would of course be five minutes. Inside of this was hinged a little metal triangle, which I lifted so it stood up straight from the dial. At one side, a little compass was set in the box.

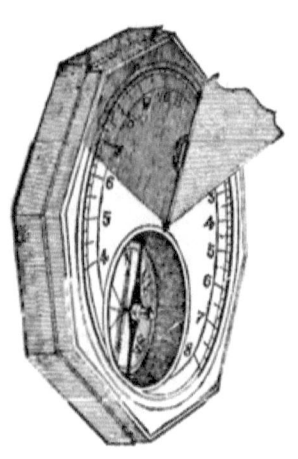

"Trim boat, Joe!" and we moved so as to bring her level on the water; then I set my box on the thwart, and shifted it about till the compass needle lay exactly over the printed north-and-south line, and noted where the edge of the shadow cast by the triangle cut across the figures.

"Twenty-five minutes past six!" I announced.

"That's very nice; have you any idea how near right it is?"

"I've tried it lots of times by the town clock; and it's never more than ten minutes out of the way."

"Where'd you be if the sun was clouded over?"

"I never had any reason to try it then!"

At the time I woke that morning it wouldn't have told me anything; but now it came in just right; and Joe condescended to regulate his paragon of a chronometer by it.

By half-past seven we had caught only three more; but we stowed our tackle and moved off. There was no promise of rainy weather as yet, notwithstanding the moon; the sun glared fiercely from both sky and water, and we were glad to get in the shade of the woods again.

Soon Camp Luna came in sight, with a little smoke still rising from our fire up at the ledge; the expedition stopped a minute to get its blankets, and then moved onward into the unknown.

Our river now changed its character, and became freaky; we couldn't depend on it for three minutes together. First we would come on a round, still pool, with the brown water black in the middle, and like as not twice over your head; then would come a shallow, gravelly stretch, with the current rushing so that it was hard work to rush the boat along, and we both had to put in and shove. It crooked oftener, along here; and there was no knowing what the next bend might open to us.

One of these pools was a beauty; bigger than the others, with a steep rock on one side rising higher than the water, crowned with tall trees, and draped in front with creepers trailing down to the stream which was black as ink in the shadow; but opposite the rock it shoaled up bright brown, over a shelving sandy bottom that sloped up to a little white sand beach, between the water and the grass.

This was a prime place for a swim, and we were all ready for it; for the day was turning out to be pretty hot, and we had been taking considerable exercise shoving over the shallows.

We had a grand time splashing around; and we sounded and found it was as much as eight feet under the rock, with a sandy bottom; so Joe went 'round to the top of the rock — it wasn't quite twice his height from the water — and took a "header."

He brought up some of the bottom — bright, white sand, same as the shore. He said he saw one of my scorpions down there, half as long as my arm; of course I knew he was "fooling," but I had forgotten all about that crawfish, and it made me feel rather "crawly." So pretty soon I came out; and Joe followed.

We didn't put on our shoes and stockings, for we said the next shallow we came to, we'd get out and tow her; and that was a good idea, for the next was a long one, and wide too; and the channel was sometimes on one side, sometimes the other.

We got out and laid hold of the painter, and waded along; it wasn't half the work it was to shove her, only we wern't used to going barefoot, and the gravel was coarse and felt pretty knubbly, and slippery, too. At last Joe got in and put on his shoes, while I took care of the boat; he said they were old, anyway, and he might as well stamp them out this trip. Then I did the same; but she stuck fast on a shoal, and he had to wait till I got out; then she came along all right.

After this shoal, we had a stretch where we could row again. Here the woods thinned away, and we came to meadows; the stream notched in at the right, and made a cove which was covered with lily-pads all over, leaving just space enough at one side for the boat to slide by; and we counted seventeen lilies, all out. We plucked them, till we couldn't crowd any more stems down into the jug, and then set it on the bow; it was the first time the old *Triton* had sported a nosegay, and the fragrance came whiffing back to us as we rode along.

The rest of the way through the fields was narrow, with a swift current; so Joe took the painter and walked along the bank, while I took the steering oar, and kept her off-shore.

After we had progressed a few minutes in this canal-boat fashion, the stream turned to the right, and widened out into another little pond; and across the farther end ran a road, with a wall built up, and an archway in it for the passage of the water. On the nearer side of the road was a shed, and on the farther side, a little one-story house, with a steep roof.

If the arch had been much narrower, we would have had a "hard one" to get by ; — but we crowded through; and then Joe went up to the house to see how near right his watch was. When he came back he had a pound of butter, and a big loaf of brown-bread he'd bought. He said his watch was thirteen minutes fast.

"Their clock's thirteen minutes slow, you mean!"

He said he'd split the difference, and set it back six and a half minutes. That made it twenty-eight minutes to ten.

CHAPTER XX.

We hadn't gone much farther, when we heard that rushing noise that means a mill, or a fall, or both. We kept a good look out, and soon saw a tall brick chimney above the trees on the right; and when we had rounded the low point in front, with its thick clump of oaks, we beheld a confused pile of buildings, some wood, some brick; some one story, some two. From the open doors and windows came the rattle of machinery.

"Another dam to get over!" said I; but we couldn't see it yet, though, as we paddled along, we soon came to where the foamy water came spinning in at the left, from the sluice-way. We went on along the waste-water channel, which was deep and still,—scarcely any current; that showed there couldn't be much water coming over the dam. The stream filled back in here, from where it came in at the sluice-way.

A broad white belt was painted around the chimney, and on it, in black lettering, we read: "PEQUONSET PAPER MILL."

"A paper mill!" I exclaimed; "I never saw one!"

"Nor I. What d'you say to going over to it?"

"If they'll let you!"

"Well, they can't be much troubled with visitors in this out-of-the-way place, and I guess they won't mind."

So we moored the boat nearly opposite the door, and ventured in. We were at one end of a long, low room; close by was the end of a long, narrow machine, which extended away to the other end of the place; it seemed to be made up of rollers, above and below, some large, some small; but all the same length, reaching across the machine.

These rollers were all moving slowly; and around, between, and among them everywhere, was a broad band of smooth dark-blue paper. It was nearly as wide as the length of the rollers, and must have been well toward half a mile long; for all through that machine you could see it gliding this way and that, slanting down backward and slanting up forward, till at the end near us a lot of it was wound in a big roll on a sort of spool, which was turning and winding it up all the time. A dozen rolls, which had been slipped off the spool as it filled, were standing on end in the corner.

We walked to the other end, and passed a group of large rolls which shed heat around, like a stove. A young man standing near by readily explained that these rollers were hollow and heated by steam, admitted within; so that the paper was thoroughly dried as it passed over them.

We went on, and saw a blanket moving toward

us; it came slowly along, carrying the band of paper on top, till at last it turned down around a roller, the same as a belt, leaving the paper to go the rest of the way by itself, and went back underneath to the roller at the other end, where it came around up and met the paper. It could hardly be called paper, here, as it was only a thin layer of wet pulp; but it kept draining as the blanket carried it along.

Hereabouts the affair was so covered in by boards and timbers that we couldn't fix the point where the sheet took form; but soon we reached the end, where the pulp came down through a trough from the room above, and poured into a large box into which a steam pump was sending a stream of water; and over the other edge of the box the wet stuff was constantly crowding.

I asked if they made writing paper here, and the young man said no; only wrapping paper. He told us that for finer kinds a still longer machine was needed, with a wire belt as well as the blanket, and apparatus for "sizing"; the pulp also had to be finer and of better material.

We went into a room where were heaped together all sorts of old paper, envelopes, postal-cards, etc., also straw and old rope, and a bale or two of rags; all to be worked up into clean, new wrapping paper.

Adjoining this was a room at the corner of the

building, which was almost filled up with an immense round vat, three or four yards across, and rising above our heads till it almost touched the roof-beams; the place was full of steam, and smelt like washing-day, only worse. Every day was washing-day there; for in that great tub was boiled and steamed the refuse stuff which we had just been looking at.

We didn't stay here long, but went up-stairs to a big room in the second story of the main building, where was a steam-engine that wasn't going, and two more big vats; but these weren't much over a foot deep, and we could look in and see what was inside.

The one we first came to, was full almost to the edge with blue pulp, such as we had seen coming down the spout; it was a pasty, unpleasant-looking mess, like dark-blue mud; and one wouldn't think it was all ready for making into nice clean paper; but it was.

There was a sort of paddle-box arrangement in the tub; not in the middle, but close against one side, with a wheel whirling around in it, out of sight, which had knives set in the rim; the axle stood out, and carried a pulley with a belt which ran down through slits in the floor to where the power was. A man came in, and told us about it; he said the wheel sucked the pulp in at one side, and sent it out at the other, cutting it finer on the way; we could see that the whole mass was slowly making the circuit of the tub.

The other vat looked just the same, but its work was less particular; for it did the finest grinding, and the pulp was coarser. Near by was a row of barrels against the wall, which held dry-ground colors of various kinds; bright chrome-yellow, blue, green, red, and black. The color was mixed with the pulp in the second vat, or "beating-engine," as he called it. He said that the long machine which made the paper was called a "Fourdrinier," after the Frenchman who perfected it about eighty years ago.

We found that the steam-engine was used in dry times, when the stream was low; but now they were running the mill by water-power. Joe asked where the wheel was; and the man told him to look out of the window, and he could see all there was to be seen.

We did so — and there was another big vat or hogshead down below, with a spout leading to the top of it from the mill-pond; its lower part stood in the sluice-way, and the water came foaming up around it, and ran off down to the river; the wheel was inside, out of sight. He said it was a "turbine" wheel, of thirty horse power.

Then we went down another flight of stairs, which led to an outside door, close to the boiler house; there were two boilers, but only one was fired up, to make steam for the washing-vat. Nobody was there.

"This is as big as Shad Factory," remarked Joe, "and it takes only two or three men to run the whole concern!"

We turned the corner of a one-story brick "L," a storage-room, for we could see boxes and rolls of paper through the windows.

"Well," said Joe, "we've explored the paper-mill; and now we'll have to think about getting the *Triton* up into the pond. Hullo! look at that!"

He pointed to the window we were passing, and there on one of the panes was a picture — on two of them! The first was a baby, with astonished eyes and its mouth wide open, and a dress perfectly loaded with laces and flummery; and the other was a two-horse team at somebody's front door, with one man holding the horses' heads, and another on the front seat grasping the lines, with a man and woman in behind; five or six people were standing in the doorway or sitting on the steps, all looking straight at you.

It was plain enough that these were photographs, and on glass; but who'd have expected to see that kind of window-panes—especially up here, fifteen or twenty miles from everywhere!

We examined the windows as we went along, but didn't see any more till we came to the room where we first went in, and that was just full of 'em, there were plenty of windows, anyway; and some were pretty nearly half made up of pictures. It was strange we hadn't noticed them when we first came up, but then our eyes were all for the machinery. They were mainly human beings of all kinds and ages; with a few store-fronts and dwelling-houses; and there was one view of some cows in a field.

The young man saw us, and came to the door.

"Do paper-mills generally sport this kind of an art gallery, or is this one putting on more style than common?" inquired Joe.

He laughed, and said he didn't think we'd find the like anywhere else,— not as far as he knew. Then he went on and told us that a man had lately bought an interest in the concern, who had been a photographer in Boston. Now he was agent there for the mill.

Before he took hold, it hadn't been running for a spell; and some mischievous scamp had done considerable window-smashing. So this man sent down a lot of his old negatives to use in making repairs.

"Come and see how they look from inside."

So we went in again and looked through them at the sky; and it was queer enough. A man's nose and forehead would be black, and his eyes and moustache white; the trees white, and sky black, etc.;

just the opposite of what they properly were. But from outside, with the dark machinery behind, they looked all right.

"That your boat?" said our friend, coming to the door with us as we went out.

"Yes; and we'll need help to get her up into the pond. Know of anybody?"

"Jim was around here half an hour ago, but I guess he's gone home. I'll see if he's within hail."

He yelled for "Jim" two or three times, and between whiles we told him where we were from, and about our camping out, etc., and he was quite interested. He said he'd help us himself, only he couldn't leave long enough; but if we'd go up the road about a quarter of a mile we'd come to where Jim lived, and he or his brother, or both, would be willing to help us over, he knew.

CHAPTER XXI.

The mill lay between the road and the river; and a short lane branched down to it. When we were nearly through the lane, we saw a boy coming down the road; he was a little larger than either of us, and carried a long bamboo fishing-rod.

"Perhaps that's him!" whispered Joe.

He turned the corner toward us, and Joe gave a nod and asked, "Do you know anything of the whereabouts of Jim Haskell?"

"That's my brother!" he replied, looking at us curiously; "he'll be after me with the bait in a few minutes. What d'ye want of him,—you know him?"

"We thought may be you were him; so you see we're not exactly acquainted with him; but a man down here at the mill said perhaps he'd help us get our boat up to the pond, so we had just started along to find him."

"You got a boat here?" he asked eagerly. "Where did you come from — Harlow's Pond?"

"We were there this morning and got some fish, and we'd like to try our luck in the pond here; how is it — is there much worth trying for?"

"Well, not much for size; you can always get perch and 'pouts, but they're small."

Then he asked us about our luck that morning, and we told him about Joe's pickerel. By that time his brother came running up, and we were in sight of the boat.

"These fellows want us to help get their boat over into the pond."

Jim was a thick-set chap, rather smaller than either of us; he looked stout and spry, and eyed us keenly; but before he could say anything the other told him we were from Harlow's Pond, and had caught a pickerel there that morning.

"You won't get any pickerel here! you'd better have kept on there."

"Well, we thought we'd come up this way, and see what there was anyhow. It's worth the trip to see your picture-show here!"

The boys grinned. "Yes," said Jim, "we call that Charley's studio. There he is now,"—as the young man appeared at the door.

"I told these boys I thought you'd help them with their boat. It didn't take 'em long to find you!"

"If they'd waited a little, they needn't have started at all! We were on our way here. Now, Si," Jim went on, "we'd better not take this boat nearer to the dam; it's steeper banks there, and it'll be easier to carry her a longer way, where it isn't so much uphill."

So we crossed in her to the other side, and tugged

her out on the turf, where we unloaded the bags, sail and oars, etc. The boys wondered what our tent-stakes were for, so we told them; and said we intended to camp out that night, somewhere farther up.

Jim persisted that we wouldn't find better fishing anywhere above. He didn't seem to think of our going just for the fun of going.

We remembered how awkward it was, carrying her before, because there was no place where we could take hold and walk along comfortably: so now Joe brought out a new plan he had been hatching up. He led the painter across underneath, a little back of the bow, so it made a bight which he could throw over his shoulder; while I could also shoulder a loop of it on the other side. Then he cast off the anchor rope, and rigged it the same way for the other boys.

We plucked leaves and stuffed our pillows, to put under the rope so it wouldn't cut into us, and the other fellows found some bits of board which they said would answer for them.

Then we got ourselves in position and straightened up at the word; and Joe's idea worked tiptop. We walked straight ahead, and never set her down till we reached the edge of the mill-pond.

This dam was twice as high as the one at Shad Factory; there must have been quite a fall there before it was built up, but it wasn't as wide. The pond widened out from it, and was nearly round, instead of long, like the other.

The boys went back with us to help bring our things to the boat, and wouldn't think of taking any pay; but they said the only boat on the pond had been taken by Tim Conway to go up a little farther and get some lilies; they expected him back every minute, but till he came they would like to fish from our boat, if we didn't mind.

So we didn't load our things in yet, but all four of us stepped aboard, and I pulled to where they said, a little beyond the middle of the pond; the anchor just reached, but it held her, as there was hardly any wind.

We all managed to get our lines out clear of each other, but sure enough the fishing didn't seem to be as good here. The pond wasn't half the size, for one thing. Joe caught a perch and I got a bream. The others didn't do any better, for all they were used to it and had regular poles.

We didn't keep it up long, for in a little over a quarter of an hour Tim Conway came back with the boat they wanted, — a rough little tub — and after he got ashore with his lilies we rowed up to it; Jim and Si clambered in with their fish, paddled themselves out into the pond, and set to watching their floats again, while we pulled to where our goods lay on the bank, and loaded them aboard. Then we headed up and away, to see what the regions beyond had in store for us.

While we were fishing the boys had told us there was another mill — a small grist-mill — about two miles farther up; but they didn't believe we could get there, for half or three-quarters of a mile this side of it was a place where the stream spread out over a wide gravel-bed and split into several parts, all shallow.

We suggested that perhaps we could get somebody to help carry the boat around, but they said it would be a pretty long tug. Then beyond the mill it wasn't any too easy for a boat,— not after we left the pond; but that was twice the length of this one, though not as wide.

That's Glenn's Pond," said Jim, "and Hollisville's within three miles above."

We asked him how large a place that was, and he said it was all along one street — the Woodfield 'Pike; there were two churches, a store and post-office and a blacksmith's shop. And Silas was telling us about some kind of cave in the rocks not very far ahead, on the right hand side, only it was in thick woods, and we couldn't see it from the stream.

"But there's a tree lying across — come to think, you'll bring up against it."

"We'll see about that!" put in Joe.

"O yes; you can get around by — well, there's a kind of trail leading across where that tree is, — not very plain, but I guess you can make it out, — and it goes right to the rocks."

He went on, how he had " heard tell" that somebody killed a bear in that den a good while ago and I asked if it was since he was born.

"Massy, no!" laughed Jim; "'twas four or five hundred years ago."

"Then it must have been Indians did it!" declared Joe.

Silas told Jim he'd better keep his clapper shut, and not let folks find out he didn't know nothin'.

"'Twasn't no Injuns did it," he said, "'twas one of the old settlers, 'way back, some time before the Revolutionary War."

But he didn't know any particulars,—that was all he could tell us about it.

We pulled out of the pond, and into a woodland patch which cut off our view of it; but first we waved hats to the boys, and they waved back. After a few minutes in the shade, we came on a place where the stream widened out, and was covered with lily-pads, except a narrow channel winding through the middle; but there were no flowers— only buds; Conway had made a clean sweep.

The stream was deep along here, but not very wide, just about room for the oars; the current was tolerably strong, and we didn't get ahead very fast. Here and there were notches and nooks where little crowds of shiny black water-beetles were spinning about. We were now in the fields again; but we saw woods about half a mile northeast, and concluded that the cave must be there. Our winding course led us there at last, after a long, hot pull against the current.

We were glad to get into the shade once more, for it was the hottest weather we had explored in; I was rowing, and thought of getting out and resting a while under the trees, but Joe persuaded me to push on as far as the cave. He said we'd make a long halt then, and he'd take the oars after that.

Those were pleasant woods; big trees and not much undergrowth, it was so shady. A rabbit jumped away from close by us; the sunbeams straggled down across the trunks here and there, and he'd keep coming in sight as he bounded through those bright places, and then we'd lose him again—but in ten seconds he was gone for good.

"I wish Harry Burrows would have let me take his revolver!" exclaimed Joe, "we'd have had rabbit for supper."

I didn't see at all that his having had a revolver along would have been likely to make any difference about our supper. But I only remarked that the rabbit must have been to the water to drink.

"Rabbits never drink!" said Joe; but I told him these wild rabbits were quite different from the tame ones, which came from Europe in the first place; these were really hares; and I didn't believe anybody could say *they* didn't drink, for I never heard of one being tamed.

Joe didn't make any reply to that, for he'd caught sight of the tree across the stream, just ahead. It was a good-sized tree, and had been there a good while; for the limbs were dead, and mostly broken off. The spot where it had grown was several feet from the water, so that the main part of the trunk lay up ashore; and where it reached the stream, it began to branch out.

If it hadn't been for that, we might have crowded under; but some of the old stumps of branches stuck down into the water, and barred our way. 'Twas an awkward thing to get around, for the trunk stretched well in shore on one side, and the snaggy top about as far on the other.

The limbs on the upper side were gone, so one could walk over without any trouble; and we concluded the best way would be to try and haul the boat over, close to the east bank, where the tree was smooth, and not more than a foot above water. But I was tired; and we made up our minds to leave that job till we got back from the cave.

CHAPTER XXII.

We found the path leading up from the tree, where the dead leaves and slender weed-stalks showed signs of trampling, and followed it along easily, over plenty of big toadstools, bright red on top, and several unripe puff-balls; we broke some of these open, and they did look good enough to eat — so white and meaty; but we knew toadstools were decidedly unwholesome, to say the least, and likely enough the puff-balls were too; at any rate, we didn't care to be the first to try.

But — what was more interesting — I noticed some stalks of "Indian pipe," which I had only seen once before; and Joe had not seen it at all. It seemed like a sort of ghost-plant — so white all over, stalk, leaves, and flower — and its whole substance is like potato-sprouts in a cellar.

The name fits well; for it's shaped very like pictures I've seen of old Indian calumets; the leaves fringe around in regular rows like the feather trimmings, and the flower curves over like the bowl. I gathered some, and I wished I could keep them that way; but of course they wilt — and there's another curious thing; they turn browner and browner, till when they're dried up, they're almost jet-black, same as a proof from the photographer's.

"INDIAN PIPE."

We found ourselves walking up hill, and there were rocks showing ahead between the tree-trunks, but we didn't see the cave till we got there, for it wasn't on the side toward us. There was no hole in the rock; it was where a huge boulder had fallen partly over and partly against the ledge; 'twas a pretty respectable cavern, though, to look at from outside; with an opening almost as big as the side of a room, and dark as pitch in back.

Well, in we went, of course; and in a few moments we found the roof come sloping down, so we had to stoop — in the course of twenty paces we were bent almost double. Joe said we were running it into the ground; and I told him it would run *us* there, if we kept on.

But we saw a gleam of light from the left — and there was a split in the ledge which we could squeeze through; and we were in a sort of entry-way a few feet long, where we could stand upright. There was a crack in the roof where some light sifted through, and a sunbeam struck in at the farther end, where there was a thick bed of dry leaves, whirled in by the wind.

When we got there, we could see outside, and a few steps brought us around the end of the ledge; but this entrance was narrow, and trees grew up, so you mightn't notice it unless you knew it was there.

Then we went back through the other way, which was more effective,—squeezing through that narrow slit into the big chamber, with that wide opening before us; and we wished we had come that way first. We wondered in what part the bear lived, and which way the man came in for him; and agreed that if we were hunting him we'd rather be in the narrowest part, where he couldn't jam through. Then we could dodge either way, while he was running around outside from one entrance to the other; and we'd be peppering him all the time, whichever way he came.

Then we clambered to the top of the ledge. 'Twas getting along toward noon; it had hardly seemed like it in the woods, it was so shady; but the rocks made a break in the trees, and there were spaces where the sun came down bright and hot, so I could hardly bear my hand on the rock.

We began to feel hungry, and it wasn't long before we started for the boat again. There she was, on the down-stream side of the tree; I wished she had sense to crawl over of her own accord, but that was too much to expect, even of the *Triton*.

So after lightening her, we perched on the log, and braced ourselves to the painter; and after a deal of tugging and swaying, we got her nose up across. Then Joe went ahead with the painter, while I pushed at the stern; fortunately there was a stone near the shore, with its top just above the surface, where I could get a tolerable footing.

By united straining we forced her up and across,

'TWAS A PRETTY RESPECTABLE CAVERN, THOUGH, TO LOOK AT FROM OUTSIDE.

a few inches at a time; but the farther she went, the worse it was for me, for I was obliged to reach out forward, and rest part of my weight on the boat, to keep balanced. Then Joe had to give a tug before I was ready, and he swung her 'round enough to throw me off.

Of course I hung on desperately; while Joe was startled, and let up on his end;—so she came launching back and slumped down with me trailing underneath, still hanging to the stern! I thought he would split; but then it never did take much to tickle Joe. "Now we're even!" he cried. "Every time we pull across a log, one of us has to go under!"

I told him 'twas his turn next; and he said he'd bear it mind, next one we came to. Then he wanted to begin over again, and I refused to unless he took the stern;—the fact was, I had a different plan in mind.

Joe wasn't anxious for the change, after seeing how it worked with me; he declared I couldn't get any wetter; and I reminded him that his turn to fall in didn't come till the next log. Finally, I showed him that by taking the hatchet and chopping off a couple of the limbs that branched down into the water, we would have room to go underneath.

That suited him; so I cut away one, then he tackled the other, and in five minutes the *Triton*, with all her belongings, was on the up-stream side. And now we could come back without any further work; while the other way, it would have been as much trouble the second time as the first.

Now we sat down and had dinner; the brown-bread tasted first rate, and we finished the loaf; I opened my can of salmon, and each of us ventured to add one of the ten-minute eggs.

Then Joe took the oars, according to agreement; and I aided with an occasional shove from the steerman's seat. I felt pretty damp; but at least I was also comfortably cool.

The woods lasted for quite a spell, but it was easy progress most of the way; no brush sticking in from the banks, and a moderate current. After we left the woods, the stream was narrower, and often we both had to stand up and urge her along by pushing.

We saw a long twig standing out a yard from the surface, that acted as though it was alive — it kept twitching backward and forward as regularly as machinery. Joe's first notion was that a fish had tangled at the bottom; but no fish would have kept it up steadily, that way. He knew that, and was rather puzzled; but I soon saw it was much the same thing as the "sawyers" on the western rivers, which I had read of.

"It's this way," I told him; "the current bends it over till the spring of the twig gets stronger than the force of the water; then the switch jerks back to where it relaxes enough for the current to urge it forward again. First it submits, and then rebels when the strain is more than it can stand."

I went on and said that the brass "reed" in the fish-horn or accordion went the same way, only a deal faster, of course. And as it turned out he hadn't heard of the "sawyer," I gave him some light on the subject, too.

"They're big trees that fall into the river, when the bank caves away; and after floating down a while, they get caught against the bottom by the roots, and the top lays down-stream. The current plays against them, and forces them slowly down out of sight; but by-and-by they get to the 'sticking-place,' and then they come slowly rearing up again.

"I've read that the flatboatmen used to hate them worse than 'most anything. They'd be sweeping 'round some bend — at night, perhaps — with the river all clear ahead; and all at once a great scraggy tree-top'd come shaking and dripping up right in front of them like a thousand-legged sea-monster, and smash they'd go into it — get stoved or capsized, like as not!"

"And they call 'em sawyers because they keep bowing down and straightening up, like a man sawing cord-wood, I suppose. See! there's a cardinal-flower."

There it was, glowing away like a coal of fire, at the water's edge. We soon came in sight of several more, scattered along the bank, and just blazing among the green grass. Joe said he wished he could get some red paint as bright as that.

"Would you paint Pierhaven red?"

"Not quite;" he laughed. "But I'd put a streak around the old *Triton* that'd knock the spots out of Walt Gurney's *Teaser*, and everything else in the harbor!"

CHAPTER XXIII.

Now there came a place where the bank was clear for some ways; and I got out with the painter and towed, while Joe steered. But soon the bushes grew up close again, and I had to give that up. We had a hard time getting her along now, with both current and branches hindering us, until we struck a gravelly shallow, where the channel was wider.

This could not be the bad place we had been told of, for there was water enough to float the boat and us too; but we got out and waded, towing her along by the painter, because it was easier.

Soon we found a lot of bigger stones scattered along the bed of the stream, large as paving stones and larger, so that the boat scraped some of them; the banks grew steeper, and the water narrower and deeper, till it was almost to our knees, and we had to stop wading.

The current was swift, and it was as much as we could do to make any headway; so I went ashore, though the trees were pretty thick, and by tying the rope around my waist, and using both my hands to work my way past the trunks and branches, we got a few rods farther up. At last a tree branched across so thickly that I had to take to the boat again. We grasped the limbs and pulled ourselves by.

Here was a bend; and when we rounded it there were the shallows sure enough! a broad stretch of sand and gravel, with two separate streams curving about over it.

In a minute or two we came to the fork, and turned into the larger stream; there was plenty of room to walk on either side, so I took the painter out on the right, and Joe took the anchor rope on the left, and on we went at a fairly good rate. This lasted only a little while; then the water spread out wider, and the boat began to scrape the bottom; soon it was so shallow, we had hard work pulling her.

We let go and walked ahead a little to see how things looked. In a few rods the streams united, and the water was a foot deep; farther on the gravelly bed made a curve which we didn't go around then, but went back to fetch up the boat. I caught hold astern and pushed, while Joe towed; when we came to a hard place, I'd pull upward and lift some of her weight, and so ease her over. In this way we reached the point where the streams joined, and then we towed on around the bend without any trouble.

But again the water divided, and the boat began to scratch gravel once more. Still we persevered, though we knew there couldn't be much paint left on the poor *Triton's* bottom; I could see bright green patches of it on the larger pebbles, as I urged her onward.

This gravelly region didn't wind about as much as some places we'd been over, and the bends weren't sharp; still there was no time when we could see very far ahead; and so all at once we were surprised to find our branch dividing again, and there was no getting farther by either way.

We knew the other branch hadn't divided; it had been flowing along at our left, sometimes close under the shrubby bank, sometimes along the middle, and once or twice almost meeting our branch.

We walked on quite a distance, to take another survey,— and the stream we had been following divided still again, and went straying about in three different channels; the water slipped and rippled over the gravel very prettily, but we had no use for these cunning little streamlets.

The other, or left branch, seemed to still hold its own; — though there was less water in it than the other had held at its best; and we and the *Triton* knew there wasn't enough in that.

"We must get to that next pond, anyway!" declared Joe; and I felt the same way. So we returned to the boat, and unloaded our things on the gravel, then pulled her across to the other branch; and we had little more trouble in getting her up that, than on the other with her load in. After taking her up a little way, we stopped a few moments to get the bags and blankets and put them in again, leaving the oars, sail, and tent-fixings; then on we scraped. It was tedious business; but we hoped it was as much as half through with.

We got beyond where our first branch split into three; and after awhile one of those came into ours, or rather ran out of it, so the first branch was partly made of an offshoot from this one! This made it a little easier — but soon the miserable rivulet was behaving worse than ever.

It split into two equal branches; and ahead, in plain sight, it divided still again, and there were five streams meandering about over that gravel-bed, which was there about four rods wide!

We left the boat, and followed the concern up, and it was just crazy. The water crooked all about, running together and splitting apart, making long irregular islands; sometimes there would be quite a decent depth in some one channel, but it wouldn't last any time.

"It looks too much like the head of navigation!" I muttered.

Joe made no reply, but looked rather grim; presently he said, "Let's see how far this goes, anyway!"

So we plodded on over the gravel. There were woods on each side; sometimes tall, sometimes scrubby; we kept in the shade as much as we could, for the stones were just baking in the sun. First we'd be on an island, then "mainland"; when a streamlet crossed our path, we waded through and kept straight ahead.

At last the branches came together in one, which was broad and rather shallow, and flowed rapidly over gravel; still it was deep enough for us. Between there and the boat, though, was all that desolation, scarcely better than dry land; she was little more than half-way through this miserable region.

"We might walk up to the mill, and ask 'em to open the sluice and let some of the pond water down here," I suggested.

"That'd wash us down to the paper-mill!" said he.

"Oh no! a little wouldn't; and we don't need——"

"Hold on a minute!" he interrupted; and I saw he was in a "study." Then he brightened up. "I think we'll get her here!" he said. "The head of navigation isn't nearer than Glenn's Pond, yet!"

"It'll take all the afternoon!" I declared.

Joe pulled out the inevitable timekeeper.

"I'll bet this," he announced impressively, "that we'll float here — *float* here, inside an hour!"

"Don't!" I replied, "I wouldn't take it from you!"

"Twenty minutes to one," he went on. "Hurry along back, and I'll tell you!"

He strode along at nearly a run, saying, "Your talking about filling up here from that pond, put it into my head. We can have a pond of our own! Just put a dam below this stuff, where it's narrow—there are those big stones, just the thing—and there you are!"

"Joe, you've hit it again!" I cried. "Ain't I glad I took you along!"

"All we want," he pursued, "is three or four inches more depth in these runlets; and it won't take long to do that, with the amount of water there is coming down."

We were both delighted with the idea, and hurried on, skipping across the rivulets. Here lay our boat, seemingly at the end of her voyage.

"We'll soon change all that!" I panted.

"Yes! the *Triton's* farthest north is yet to be recorded!" he uttered majestically.

When we reached the narrows, we had to leave the margin of the stream, because of the thick bushes along the bank; we were a little confused by the dense shrubbery clumps, and got farther from the river than we intended; so that we were several minutes in finding it again, and struck it farther down than the place we had in mind.

We were at the point where the stream first widened out and showed a gravelly bottom; but it didn't take long to wade up to the big stones, and what we had to do was to carry these up to where the narrows were, with high banks on either side.

This was no easy job; for before we got there, the water grew so deep we had to dump them on the bank, to be carried where we wanted them afterward. It was more fun than towing the boat, however; for we were "stealing a march" on our perverse river again, as we did at the peninsula. The heaviest stones we "toted" along without lifting them out of the water; as you know, this took from their weight as much as a "piece" (so to speak) of water their size would weigh.

When we had piled quite a heap, we began throwing them in where we had decided the dam should be, on each side, leaving a place in the middle to be filled up last. Before any of our work showed out of water, we had to go back for more stones; this time we brought smaller ones, as we had used up the big ones for the foundation; and soon our dam was built up to the surface on each side.

We found it would have been better to use the small ones first, for, now that the passage was partly filled, the water poured with double power through the room left to it; and our stones were rolled and trundled out of the way almost as fast as we threw them in. We saw that would never do; we were wasting time and materials; but Joe was equal to this difficulty also.

"Pity we hadn't thought to fetch the hatchet

along!" he said, "but I guess we can make out without going back for it."

Then we set out to cut down a few young trees with a jack-knife. This isn't so hard to do as you might think, "if you only know how." Perhaps you do know; but anyway it'll do no harm to tell. If the tree is slender enough for you to bend sharp over, the rest is as good as done.

We picked out some young hickories, one to two inches thick, and pulled one over till its top lay on the ground; the bent place may have been a foot and a half from the roots. Then I brought the knife to bear on the upper side of the bend, and in a second 'twas three-quarters of the way through, as though 'twere cutting cheese!

You see the "philosophy" of it was this: the knife didn't get *wedged*. It's always easy enough to cut into the surface; it's after that the trouble begins; but here it was surface right along, for the strained fibers drew apart out of the way, and there wasn't any packing. I needn't say, though, that your knife should have an edge several degrees sharper than a hoe.

The cut wouldn't go quite through, so we bent it the opposite way, after a little bother from the top getting against the other trees; then we finished the cut from the other side. We divided this and two others into lengths of about four feet each, in the same way, bending them around the trunks of larger trees.

Of course, the idea was to build these in across the opening, so as to hold the stones with which we filled up afterward. Joe had to take off his clothes, and go right in, so as to get at it properly; of course he didn't mind that, but he found it hard to brace against the current, and was washed off his feet once or twice.

I handed him the stakes, and he built them across, one above the other, like a rail-fence, the ends stuck among the stones on either side. Then he took smaller sticks, as big as your finger, and wove them in and out among the others so as to make a grating.

Now we made a final collection of stones and heaped them up on the bank; when we judged there were enough, we dumped them in behind the grating, as fast as we could. Soon the water began to rise and flow over on each side, and wash the smaller stones off the top of the dam; so we stopped and spent some time in hunting for the biggest stones we could get. We found several around on land, so heavy it took both of us to carry them; but when he had laid them on our work, and "chinked up" the spaces between with smaller stuff, it was too much for the water at last.

A regular torrent rushed through the grating, though, so we were afraid it would part from its moorings; but it didn't; and we finished filling in behind it, bringing the heap of stones up level with the top stake, and finished the construction with our two biggest stones, square flat affairs three or four inches thick. These made the lip over which the the stream would pour, for the sides were a trifle higher; we saw that the water would yet rise more than a foot, here; and when it had ponded back half that in the upper channels, we would be all right.

CHAPTER XXIV.

So now we trudged back to await results; and first thing, here came the oars and sail floating slowly down to meet us! We had left them just at the water's edge.

We fished them out; I took the oars and Joe the sail;—of course we had to laugh at the thing; but presently Joe said it was no joke carrying that wet sail, it was equal to so much lead; so he took one of the oars, and we each laid hold of an end of the mast and carried it between us.

We passed the place where we had left them, and the water there was half-way to our knees;—it had hardly been over our feet before. Then we hurried up; for we didn't want to find the *Triton* sliding back, after the trouble we'd had to get her where she was.

The water in the channels was getting lower and flowing swifter, as we went on; and before we came in sight of the boat we were beyond where the effect of our dam was felt, as yet, so we slackened our pace; for we were regularly "tuckered" out.

When we reached the *Triton*, we let the things fall, and dropped flat on the sand, in the shade. We were rather glad the water hadn't risen yet, so we had an excuse for waiting and doing nothing;

and we had worked hard enough the last two hours to have earned a little rest.

We lay spread out there without speaking or moving a finger. It was right comfortable, on the soft, dry sand, looking up at the spots of sky shifting between the leaves, only it was rather dazzling to my eyes, and I shut them now and then, to give them a rest.

In a minute or two I heard Joe muttering something. "What's that?" asked I.

"Guess you dropped off, didn't you?"

"No, I'm wide awake. But, all the same, I don't feel like being disturbed."

"Hear anything?" he went on.

"I hear *you*, plain enough."

"Nothing else?"

I heard the little insect hum and scraping there always is, but he couldn't mean that; and there wasn't wind enough to make a noise in the trees. I thought it was a pretty still day. Before I spoke again, he added, "Seems to *me* its uncommon *still*."

Then it came into my head what he was driving at. He meant what *didn't* I hear. I didn't hear the water rippling over the gravel.

I raised up and looked around; the stream was crawling at a tortoise rate, and the water had risen a little, but the *Triton* wasn't afloat yet.

"The dam's doing the business!" exulted Joe.

"It's beginning to rise here now! It's taken rather longer than I expected, though—twenty minutes since we got here."

I concluded that I must have "dropped off" after all.

"It's close on a quarter of two," he went on; "you've won the watch."

"Sure enough!" said I, "hand over!"

"Certainly!" he replied solemnly. "I always act up to my contracts!" and he delivered the precious machine. Of course I had no idea of keeping it.

"Now, having—ah—fully discharged my—ah—obligations, I would respectfully intimate that I have under consideration—to—ah—the purchasing of the same."

"Ah, indeed!"

"And if you're open to an offer, I would be happy to—ah——"

"Of course; anything in reason!"

"To enter on negations — negotiations, I should say."

"All right — only don't drive too hard a bargain."

"I hereby offer the sum of one cent, cash down ——"

"Gracious! take it, and my blessing! I'd no idea you valued it so highly! But 'tisn't business-like to make such a big offer, the first time. If you could be—ah — prevailed on to exchange this truly munificent sum for a rectangle of your sticking-plaster, to apply to where I've barked this knuckle——" and, with his gracious assent, this momentous matter was settled.

Our boat was afloat now, except where one cobble-stone touched her amidship; but we walked ahead, and found the maze of channels took up so much water that it wasn't best to go on quite yet. When we got back she was floating clear; but we had taken care to put the anchor over, so she didn't drift.

Joe picked up a couple of stones, and tried throwing them up from one hand, first one and then the other, keeping one in the air all the time; and he could do it pretty well; — but when he tried it with three, he got muddled. George Myers could keep it up with two from each hand, at the same time, and three with his left hand alone;—but then he was the head juggler among the boys in everything; he could keep a chair balanced on his chin for two minutes.

At last we were off! pulling our boat through the winding channels, which were so hopeless-looking a little while before, and not often did she scrape;—and weren't we glad when we came to where all met, and we could embark once more! Our dam hadn't got through serving us yet; for it slackened the current, so we could make better headway. We hoped it would last till we came back; at any rate it wasn't likely it would crumble away enough to keep us long repairing it.

As we moved up, the current told against us more and more; at last we gave over rowing, and Joe pushed astern, while I stood in the bow.

"Hold on!" I said, suddenly, and brought her nose to the bank.

"What's the matter?"

"See that frog! there on the sand, at the edge of the water!"

"My stars! what a whopper! regular old bull, isn't he?"

"Now just hold her here, till I catch him!"

"Till he dives—all right!"

So I crept out and stole along the bank; I really didn't expect to catch him, but I did! Whether he was asleep, or hadn't ever seen human beings, and wasn't afraid—he didn't stir any more than a stone, till I fairly grabbed him. Then he gave a wiggle, and his hind-legs slipped through, but his feet stuck, they were so big! till I got him secure with my other hand.

He was as heavy as a kitten, and as large; I'd never seen anything like it, neither had Joe. He didn't struggle much while we looked him over; he might have got away if he'd tried, for we handled him gently. Such broad webs on his feet! he must have been able to swim like a streak.

Joe said the hind-legs were as good as chicken. I knew they were sold in the city markets; but I didn't want to harm the big, harmless chap, so we sat him on the thwart all ready to jump, and let go; off he went, and plunged out of sight five or six feet away. It didn't seem much of a jump for a frog of his size; Joe said he was old and rheumatic, may be.

Not long after this we came to where a stream flowed in. It wasn't a "fork," for the main stream went right ahead, and this joined at right angles. A pretty little brook, this was; coming down a long slope at the right; there were tiny falls in it every few feet, where it rippled down among stones and the big roots of trees that stretched in; we could see it gleaming here and there away up to the woods on the ridge.

If it came from a spring up there, it must have been a good sized one; but we'd stopped so long on that gravelly place, we didn't want to take the time to look for it. On tasting the water we made up our minds it was better than what we were floating on; so we took our lilies from the jug, where we'd kept them all this time, and arranged them in a tin cup; then we filled the jug from the brook. Joe untied the cork from his line, and screwed it in tight; our fishing poles we had thrown away soon after leaving the paper-mill, as they cluttered the boat, and we could cut others any time.

Big clouds were drifting over the sky, and hid the sun considerable of the time; we were glad of that, for it was hot work fighting up against the current,—which was running more rapidly than ever,— and slow work, too; it was well toward three o'clock when we reached Glenn's Pond.

First, another little rivulet came slipping in, then pretty soon we heard the rush of water ahead. The land rose steeply on our right, to more than twice as high as our heads, making a grassy ridge, with trees growing thickly along the top. They were thick on the other side, too, so we couldn't see ahead, though the noise of the fall was so loud we knew it must be close by—and the water was foamy, too.

In another minute we were beyond the trees with the dam right in front, and quite a big sheet of water pouring over it, making a handsome fall; there was a bridge running across above it, but never a sign of a mill!

We brought her bow ashore, and hastened up, and there lay the pond smooth and bright before us, with woods around most of it; and to our right was the mill—the ridge had hidden it from us while we were coming up.

It was a queer looking affair for a mill, three stories high, with a sort of balcony or piazza across the end, at the top story, and the roof propped out over it. At the other end, the building backed against the ridge which held in the pond, and you could walk right into the upper story. Little dormer windows with railings stood out on the roof on each side.

A trough came out of the bank, and carried the water to the top of the wheel, which wasn't turning, though a little was running through; it must have been leakage. It dropped through into another trough, from which it ran into a channel that led off through the grass; and now we knew where that rivulet came from which we had seen just before.

The upper part was fitted up as a dwelling-house, that was easy to see; there were curtains at the windows and we got glimpses of furniture inside; but nobody seemed to be around. We knocked, and then again; and an old lady came to the door, who eyed us rather sharply at first; but when we

IT WAS A QUEER LOOKING AFFAIR FOR A MILL.

began to talk, and told her we'd like help to get our boat into the pond, she was pleasant enough.

She said we'd find Mr. Odell in the lower story, if we'd go around to the other end. We thanked her, and started; but when we had gone a few steps she called to us that there he was, coming up the road. So we turned, and went to meet him.

He was a heavily-built man, with spectacles and a good-natured look; had on a blue shirt and white overalls, and an old felt hat; his face was fringed with gray hair all around.

He stepped up to the bridge over the dam, and looked down at our boat.

"I don't see how you ever got her up as far as this," he observed. "Came by the stream, didn't ye?"

"Well, yes!" answered Joe, with a smile, "she doesn't row easy on dry land!"

"No; but I thought you might have fetched her across on a cart. Didn't you find a place below here that wasn't much better than dry land?"

"Yes," said I, "we had a hard time of it hauling her through there; but we unloaded her, and she doesn't draw much water, you see."

I didn't know whether it might be best to say anything about our dam; perhaps he felt as though he owned all the rights of that sort, thereabouts. But Joe took it on himself to out with the whole thing,— and the idea seemed to strike his fancy ; he took much more interest in us after he heard that.

"Want to fish up in here? I can't catch much."

" No ; we want to see how far we can go up with a boat."

He feared we wouldn't find it "very good sailin'," and wanted to know how far we had come.

" Well, well ! Well, well !" he said, when we told him. He'd been there fifteen years, and had never known a boat to come there from tide-water before. This was pleasant for us explorers to hear ; but we were in a hurry to get on, and again asked if he knew of any one near by who would help with the boat. We couldn't expect an old man like him to tackle such a job, that hot day; besides it took four to carry her, by our way of looping ropes.

But he told us to come along with him to the basement of the mill, where we found three good-sized wooden rollers. So the *Triton* was to travel in still another way.

Each of us carried one to where the boat lay ; and soon she was moving slowly and surely along, with Mr. Odell pushing behind, Joe pulling in front, and I taking the rollers from the rear, and laying them in place ahead. This was where the real work came in ; and I was glad when we halted, where the meadow, sloping up, met the road from the bridge at a "bar-way." In working her along the road, Joe took the rollers and I the painter.

When the *Triton* was launched again, and we had carried the rollers back, he made us come up into the house and have some milk and doughnuts, while he gave his wife an account of what we had told him. She brought out some white bread and honey; and while we were eating it she packed a paper bag with doughnuts and cheese for us to take along, and the thanks we returned were sincere.

"I suppose we'll see you again before long," said he, as we embarked, "for you'll have to come back the same way."

"Yes; and I'm sorry we'll have to trouble you again so soon!"

"No trouble; not a bit!" he answered, heartily.

"They're the right sort!" asserted Joe, as we rowed away.

CHAPTER XXV.

We didn't stop here to try for fish. We'd fished in two ponds, already, since we set out that morning, and we wanted to get on; this was the afternoon of our third day, and we were still on navigable waters.

The boys at the paper-mill had told us this pond was longer than the one there; but it seemed to us about the same size,—a little smaller, if anything. It didn't take five minutes to get to the end, where a wooded point came down from the left, matching the woods across so you could hardly see where the the stream came in, till you were nearly there.

But when we had entered it, making a short turn to the left around the point, we found it was wide,—three boat-lengths at least.

We found more,—it wasn't any stream at all! It was where the pond narrowed for a few rods; then it opened out into twice as long a stretch as the first. This was a lovely pond; the woods went part way, then gave place to meadows, with trees growing along the fences, and scattered about; near the farther end was a big farm-house, the main part white, with an "L" painted red, with white trimmings. There were two barns; the larger had a cupola, which in turn was crowned by a windmill.

Between the barns was a cart-shed, one end of which was inclosed for a hen-house and showed plenty of window-sash.

When we came to the inlet where the stream flowed into the pond, there was a lane or cart-path leading down from the barns, and fording right across; the water wasn't more than a foot deep, at that place. Beside it, a little rill came sparkling down.

Just ahead a log was lying across, hewn flat on top, to serve as a foot-bridge. We thought maybe we could jam the *Triton* through under this; so we both stood on the gunwale at each side of the bow, resting our hands on the log, to keep our balance, and so we got the bow under, the stern rising a little, however, to make up. We stepped backward by degrees as we urged her under, with our feet on the edge; but after grinding unwillingly about four feet, she came to a dead halt. The farther she went, the wider she was where the log held her down, and the harder she pressed up against it.

We thought, of course, of hauling her on shore and around it; but we would have to unload her, and we preferred to manage it with less trouble, if we could. The next idea was to lift one end of the log; Joe was the stoutest, so I got the painter under, and carried it up the bank, ready to haul when he raised the log. But he could scarcely stir it; and no wonder, for it was as much as fifteen feet long.

We both tried; and by tugging savagely we did pull it up a few inches,—when the *Triton* slipped from under and began drifting backward, so we let drop and grabbed the painter. The sweat was dripping from both our faces.

"If there was only somebody to haul her along while we lifted!" exclaimed Joe. "I'll tell you— we might drive a stake ahead and lash our pulley to it, with the painter rove through; then may be I could gather it in with my toes, while we lifted."

I had to laugh at that, and so did he.

"You're too ingenious!" I said, "you'd have to be more of a monkey than you are, to do that. What we want to do is, to set up a block or something to shift the log on; then we can take our time about getting her through?"

Before we could turn to look for something of the sort, somebody behind us hailed, "What you fellers tryin' to do?—want to get your boat through?"

'Twas a tall young chap who looked as though he might be seventeen years old; he had on a blue- and-white checked shirt and "pepper-and-salt" trowsers, and wore a brown straw hat.

"That's just what we'd like!" says Joe. "If you'll help me lift this, you'll do us quite a favor."

He stepped up without a word more; and they picked it right up and held it, while I hastily pulled the *Triton* to the upper side. We could see he was a stout fellow, and no mistake; he didn't seem to mind it at all,

"I used to have a boat in this pond," he observed. "Last winter I kept her out too long, and she froze in; and when the thaw came the ice broke up in the night, and she parted her rope and slipped over the dam;— that was the last of her. You fellows must have had a hot pull of it to get your boat up from down there!"

We saw a younger boy trotting down the lane; he slowed into a walk as he saw we were not likely to get away before he came up.

"So we did; Mr. Odell was good enough to help us around, or we could hardly have managed it."

"How far've you come,— from the paper-mill?"

"We've been there to-day; but this morning we were at Harlow's Pond."

"Say!" put in the younger, "d'you know Steve McLean! he's in the spinnin' room."

"No; we're not much acquainted 'round there: we belong down below that region," said I.

"We're from Pierhaven," finished Joe, to cut short the agony.

"Hail Columby!" exclaimed the younger boy. "Where'd you strike the river?"

"We started on it from there, day before yesterday."

"You don't say!" commented the older, looking at our craft with interest.

"My! does Pequonset River go down to Pierhaven?" cried the other.

"'Course it does! why, Ben, I thought ye knowed that! So you've come all the way by water!"

"All except where the mills blocked the way. Has'nt it been done before?"

"Never, as I ever heard on; 'taint much of a place for cruisin', up this way. Where're you bound,— up to Hollisville?"

"We'd like to get there, if we can."

"Don't believe it can be done,— not this way. There's a fork about a mile above, where Beames' Brook comes in; and above that it comes tumbling down among rocks; and there's no boat that ever I see could get along in that place!"

"There's where you're right, Tom!"

"Perhaps we could get the boat carried around, same as at the mill-dams."

"Well, I don't believe you'd find ten rods together that'd float you, from there on. Still, I never tried it. But if you want to get to Hollisville,— I'm just going to catch old Dick, and drive over, to get the *Weekly Banner* and some store-truck; and I'll take you there and back, if you like;— just lief's not. Your boat'll be all right, here."

"Suppose we do!" I said to Joe.

"All right!" said he, "and much obliged to *you!*"

So we all crossed the log, and walked toward a "bar-way" a short distance to the left.

"Then this is Pequonset River, is it?" said I.

"'Course 'tis!" Ben burst out. "What d'you think

it was? H'aint you said you've been travelin' on it three days?"

"Don't be sassy, Ben! I reckon you call it something else, down there."

"Why, yes,—we call it Pierhaven River. But it's something very different, there,—salt water; and wide,—twice as wide as this pond."

Ben made a face intended to signify that I was "piling it on," but his brother didn't see him.

"I know 'taint much of a river, to see now," said Tom, "and Pequonset Brook would sound fitter; but sometimes,—in the spring, when the snow melts,—it looks pretty respectable."

"You bet!" cried Ben. "Where we've just been across, I've seen it four times as wide as the pond!"

So our story was overmatched; but Tom added, "Four times as wide as the narrow part, he means."

Here we were, at the bars; and there was old Dick, looking at us. Joe and I spread out to help head him off; but Tom caught him without any trouble; perhaps he was tired of loafing and wanted a change. As we walked along back with Ben leading the old nag, Tom said, "I don't want you to think I'm pryin', but it seems kind o' queer for you to take this roundabout fashion of getting up here. You know anybody in Hollisville?"

"No," I said, "we don't know a soul anywhere about here. We set out to follow this river up just for the fun of it, to see where we'd come out."

"D'you make a bet you'd run up to Hollisville?" asked Ben.

"No, indeed, nothing of the sort;—we wanted to find how things looked along the river, and have the fun of camping out, besides. When it won't carry our boat any longer, we'll turn back, and not before."

"I see!" said Tom, "you've been kinder *explorin'* this 'ere stream!"

"That's it, exactly."

"Well, how've you made out?—got fun enough to pay, so far?"

"Yes, we've liked it first-rate; though we've had harder work to-day, part of the time, than we'd like to do straight along."

"Yes; I reckon you must have had a tough spell of it about half a mile below here, didn't you?"

Then Joe told him about the dam we made; and he thought that was a pretty 'cute notion.

"*We've* got a dam up here a little ways——" began Ben; but his brother put in, and told him not to mind about that, now; we'd come to it in good time.

"Nothing that we can't go by, is it?"

"Huh!" said Ben, "if you got over Odell's——"

"Yes; but we didn't know but you might object."

'Aw-w no! we'll help you over!"

Old Dick splashed across, while Ben ran over the log, and caught him on the other side. As we went up toward the barn, a line of dozen geese came marching past us, in "Indian file," slow and important, with their necks stretched straight up; and their fretful "kweu kweu!" kept breaking out all along the row. The old gander had a big nub at the base of his bill; he did his level best to stretch up to our height, and looked at us out of his eye mad as fury; may be he wasn't, but all ganders look so, anyway. Ben shoved his hat at him; then he crooked his neck and jabbed out like a snake; but he failed to connect, for Ben knew him.

In the barn-yard was a trough, with water running into it at one end out of a lead pipe, which came up from the ground; there was a notch at the other end, where the overflow ran out, and made the rill which flowed down beside the lane. Tom said the water came from a spring on the hill, three-quarters of a mile off; it was brought into the house, too.

I asked if it ever failed, and he said, never quite; but in some seasons, when the brook itself was about dried up, there wouldn't be much flow from the spring; then they used the pond water for everything but drinking. We thought it a little queer that they should take the trouble to have that trough, with the pond so near; but they said it saved driving the cows down and waiting for them to drink, then turning them back into the yard.

"We mostly pasture our cows up that way,"—

pointing northwest beyond the house,—"and every minute counts, when you're tired."

When they had harnessed up, Tom went in and got his linen coat, while we helped Ben load in some sweet corn, melons and squashes. We climbed in, and Tom gathered up the reins; he wouldn't let Ben go; said there were too many things to bring back.

This was rather pleasant, for a change, jogging steadily along without having to row, shove, or tug at a rope; and we were keeping up our regular exploring, too, for we would see the stream at Hollisville farther than we could get with the boat, if we had been told aright.

After about half an hour, in which time we passed only two houses, old Dick took his own time in going up a long, steep hill; soon after reaching the top, our road was crossed by another, which was wider, and there was hardly any grass between the ruts. Tom turned down this,—he said it was the Woodfield 'Pike, and we were 'most there. There was a little yellow-brown school-house just beyond the corner, with weeds and thin grass springing up all over the trampled space around it,—then we saw a square, white cupola over the trees at the left, and Tom said that was the Baptist Church.

Three or four houses were now in sight, showing more or less; and here was a brook running under the road, through a narrow stone tunnel which was built part way across, leaving room on the left between it and the fence for teams to drive down through where the water spread out in a shallow pool, so the horses could drink.

We wanted to know if *that* was Pequonset River; and Tom said, "No," that amounted to something more than this;—this was "Beames' Brook."

The road curved to the right, and—we were at Hollisville. We passed the blacksmith's shop; a hammer was ringing from inside, where we saw a horse tethered; and a few old broken-down carts and wagons were standing around outside. The houses were mostly pleasant looking, with plenty of trees and vines, and flowers growing in front; the church, though, seemed dreadfully bare, white and dreary, with its two big doors shut up; there was a long carriage shed behind. We could see the little steeple of the "Orthodox" Church, some ways ahead.

Presently Tom drew up at the store, which had a sort of piazza roof coming out in front, held up by posts planted at the outer edge of the sidewalk. Old Dick was hitched to a ring in one of these; and then we helped carry in the "garden truck."

It was a pretty good-sized store; and it had to be to hold the things. We saw axes, ox-yokes, slates, shoes, calico, ink, sugar, flour, tinware, tea, and soothing-syrup—these just show the ground they laid themselves out to cover. The man behind the counter was quite a bright-looking young fellow,— and he must have had a good memory, anyway, to keep the run of the prices. One corner of the place was shut off with sash partitions for the postoffice, two men were sitting in there talking.

Tom told of the things he wanted; and he said to us that while they were being weighed out he was going to see a fellow who lived a little farther along; and if we cared to come part way with him, he would show us the river.

In a minute or two we came to where it went under the street, and he walked on, leaving us leaning over the railing. It would have just about floated the *Triton* here, except under the bridge; that was too narrow for her. We could see up for quite a stretch; but on the down side of the street it was in sight for only a few yards, and then turned the corner of a garden. There wasn't much of a current; a few water-spiders were drifting down on it; when they were nearly under the bridge they'd give two or three skips up-stream, and then float down again. We watched them, leaning on the rail.

"Well," said Joe at last, "it seems likely that this is our farthest. Let's see what time it is;— quarter to four, Wednesday. Seems as if we'd been longer than that!"

"Doesn't it! Well, now we'll take a farewell look."

"Let's take it from that next bend. We can keep

one eye on the bridge here, and see when Tom goes by."

So we got over the fence, and walked to where the course changed, and we could see it here and there, beyond, for some distance through the fields. At this point it grew shallower, and the grade began to slope; it came rippling and gurgling down, not more than a yard wide, in places;— it was plain that the "head of navigation," would be reached here, if not before.

"This water's going down to Pierhaven."

"Yes; but precious little it'll count for, there. I suppose it may help to make a little stronger current in the ebb-tide."

CHAPTER XXVI.

We sauntered back to the store, feeling that our expedition had reached its limit,— in one way ; still, we agreed to carry the *Triton* as far as the stream would let us, and see all we could " from the inside," as Joe expressed it.

Old Dick, moored to the post, was still nodding outside ; Tom hadn't got back yet. We bought three pounds of hard-tack, some chocolate, and ginger-snaps. Joe compared his watch with the clock, by which it was about ten minutes slow ; if this was the standard, my dial was three minutes slow,— instead of thirteen minutes fast, as it was by the clock he had seen in the morning. I told him he'd better stick to the sun-dial, and never mind these blundering clocks.

Then I took it into my head to write a letter home, and bought a sheet of paper and an envelope. Joe followed suit, and we scribbled away for three or four minutes ; then Tom appeared, so we brought our messages to a sudden close. An old man took them, and put on the stamps, then printed the postmark ; he took his time about it,— no slap-slap business such as you see in big postoffices.

He told us that the mail went every morning. We asked where, and he said " to Brompton."

"I shouldn't wonder if we'd have saved time by taking them ourselves!" I said, when we were out of hearing.

"Yes; I'd laugh if we got home first. Like as not they'll go as far as Boston before they turn this way again."

We helped Tom load his molasses, kerosene, etc., and then he started along and took us through the rest of the place and a little beyond, to where a road came in on the left. We followed this, and it turned out to be the one on which Tom lived; as we saw when it crossed the turnpike, near the schoolhouse.

Before that, we met the "river" again, still further up, where it crossed the road in a patch of woods; and it didn't look much like voyaging. It was full of mossy stones, among which it brawled and tumbled, with big rocks crowding in; we wouldn't have been sure what it was if Tom hadn't told us.

"You're right!" I admitted, "there's no getting beyond Hollisville."

"Or *to* it, in your boat; as I was a-sayin', its just as bad below, after Beames' Brook makes off."

But we told him we were bound to see it through with the *Triton*, as far as we could make her go.

As we came near the house, we saw a little church set on a pole—steeple and all, complete; with windows painted on, and holes at the doors; it looked just like the "Orthodox" Church at Hollisville. Across underneath was a little sign: "*Pews free.*"

"Pretty good!" laughed Joe, "whose work's that?"

"Well, I 'spose I can say I done it:— Bob Wardley, that I went to see to-day, marked out the letterin'. There was a pair of blue-birds in it this spring; there has been for three years back, ever since I put it up,—and I think it's the same pair."

"You must be pretty handy with tools."

"O, middlin'. I'll show you something else, before you go."

Ben came out to unharness, and I carried our purchases down to the boat. "Well, old craft,"

thought I, "you're pretty near the end, now." I took the jug up to the barn, to fill it from the pipe, and it turned out that Ben had told his mother about our expedition, and they had set out a lunch for us.

'TWAS FULL OF MOSSY STONES, WITH BIG ROCKS CROWDING IN.

We felt a little uneasy about their putting themselves to that trouble for a pair of strange boys, and hinted something of the sort; but Tom said 'twas the first boat that had come up there from salt water, and perhaps 'twould be the last; anyway, he didn't want explorers to carry back a bad opinion of people in those parts.

He showed us to the sink, so we could wash our hands; and there, instead of a pump, was a lead pipe sticking out of the wall, with a wooden stopple;—which he pulled out, and the water poured into the basin, clear, cool spring-water. If they should forget and leave the stopple out for half a day, there was no harm done; *they* never saw any water-bills.

When we finished I corked it up; but as I passed the end of the sink, out popped the plug, and took me in the face, while the stream spouted 'most a yard!—then it suddenly slackened to its usual rate.

I wondered how often their water-supply was liable to such explosions; but Tom exclaimed, "Drat that Ben! that's one of his tricks! he was watching at the trough,—out in the barn-yard; and when he saw it run harder there, he knew we'd stopped it up here; then he just clapped his hand over the spout! I've a mind to hold his head under it!"

Well, they gave us a lunch which we'll always be glad to remember them by,—huckleberry cakes, corn and beans, apple and huckleberry pie, muskmelon, and plenty of milk. Their mother was a real nice woman, and we were glad to tell her all she asked about.

We'd been wondering where Mr. Holcomb (their father) was; and it seemed that he'd gone somewhere that afternoon to look at a yoke of oxen he thought of buying; and he took the best horse, — "or I'd had you back here earlier," declared Tom.

"Tell you, *he* can *travel!*" added Ben.

Mrs. Holcomb seemed actually afraid we wouldn't eat enough; but we thought we did pretty well; especially as it was the second time we'd eaten since noon. She wondered we didn't catch cold, sleeping out of doors all night; and wanted us to stay with them till the next day,— and so did the boys; but of course we couldn't listen to that. If we didn't camp out every night we'd lose half our trip; and I think the boys saw well enough how it seemed to us; — though Tom said he'd bet anything there'd be thunder-showers that night, it was so sultry.

When we started, they made us take a quart bottle of milk, and a whole huckleberry pie in the pan; and said we could leave the pan on our way back the next day. We were really ashamed to accept them; but we couldn't get out of it gracefully,— and I don't know as we wanted to.

We all moved down to the boat, for Mrs. Holcomb wanted to see it; and Tom carried a churn—

a round one that went with a crank,—and loaded it aboard. We were astounded; but before we spoke, he laughed and said, "I aint going to give you *this*, but I thought maybe you'd let me carry it up here a little way, on your boat."

We said of course he could, and welcome; but we wondered why he should care to.

Tom and Ben wanted to get aboard and send the boat up as far as their dam; so they began to shove with their oars, one on each side, but Ben couldn't make his pushing mate with his brother's, and so they'd kept fetching around one way and the other. Then Tom told him to hold up, and let him go it alone; and he made out better.

We now took leave of Mrs. Holcomb, as she wasn't going any farther; we gave her our pond-lilies, which were still safe in the tin cup, and wished there were more of them.

Joe called to Tom that we'd take him in tow if he got tired, but he said there was no danger of that, and pushed along into the next lot, and across that into the one beyond, with us walking abreast on the bank. Then we saw their dam,— and a water-wheel a yard high, just in front and close to the bank; there was a trough for leading the water to it, which was closed by a little sliding gate.

"Is this some of your work, too?" I asked.

"Yes; you know I said I was going to show you something else."

"Well, it's done tip top! goes clear ahead of the church. Start her up,— won't you, please?"

"In a minute."

On the same same axle with the water-wheel was a solid wheel made of three round pieces of board fastened together; a leather belt connected this with another wheel below, less than half as large, which had a strip of board fixed crank fashion on its axle. Tom lifted the churn on to a little platform, and set it so its crank went through a hole in the board-crank.

Everything was plain as day, now; and we looked on with rapt attention while we lifted the little gate part way. The water poured into the buckets, and the wheel began to turn slowly; the little wheel went round four times to once of the big one, carrying the churn-crank at the same rate. It was just splendid!

Everything was finished off neatly, and painted dark-red; the dam was walled up close and even, and perfectly level on top.

"Let 'em see how fast she can go!" said Ben.

His brother pulled the gate clear up; and the big stream filled the buckets in a second; the wheel more than trebled its speed, and the churn joggled about as the crank flew around; Tom said that was too fast, so he lowered the gate till the rate suited him.

"You see I can regulate her just as I like!"

THE WATER POURED INTO THE BUCKETS, AND THE WHEEL BEGAN
TO TURN SLOWLY.

He said he'd had it going only about six weeks. They made the dam early in June, when there was a dry spell, and there wasn't as much water as now. "You'd never got up here, then," he said. The main trouble in building it was that it had to be so long,—'twas ten times as long as the one we made, for the banks didn't slope much; still they chose the best place they could find on the farm. It took the boys two weeks, what time they could get; of course laying the wall so ship-shape took some time, and then they filled in an earth-bank on the upper side, besides bracing the front with timber in several places.

Then it was quite a job setting up the wheel,— he'd made it mostly in the winter. The lengths of heavy scantling which held it up were planted five feet deep, he said; 'twould take a pretty fair freshet to wash them away — and besides, they had a sluice-gate to let the water out, when it come flooding down after rains. "It's worth the while, though; for all 'tisn't *every* time that we can fetch the churn along in a boat. She'll bring the butter in a quarter of an hour, while we have the fun of looking on."

We didn't wait for that, as it was close on five o'clock, but set to and rigged our ropes; and the four of us manned them, and got the boat up into their little mill-pond. They thought perhaps we could crowd up as far as where Beames' Brook joined, which might be a couple of miles, by the stream; 'twas a little beyond the old "Galloway place."

"If you must camp out, I s'pose you must; we'll be looking for you again to-morrow,— if you don't see us, be sure and come up to the house."

CHAPTER XXVII.

Their dam slackened the current, and made it easier for us for some time after we lost sight them.

"That Tom's a first-rate fellow!" declared Joe, "I wish he lived down at Pierhaven."

"Yes; the people here are rather different from those Frenchies at Shad Factory. I'm filled up so I don't believe I can eat anything more to-night!"

"Well our things'll keep. Hullo, though! there's our fish! we must cook them to-night, whether we eat 'em or not. That pickerel mustn't be wasted!"

"Nor the time we spent in going back to get it!"

Now a path came down to where a rock stood out of water, near the middle; on each side of it was a big chunk of stone. Somebody had put them in to step across on, for the stream widened out a little here, and was less than a foot deep.

They were too near together for the *Triton* to get between, so we rolled up our trowsers and set ourselves to trundle one or the other of them out of the way. We couldn't start either, first time trying, they were so embedded; and we thought of working her around on the sloping sandy shore. But first a little time in undermining the most promising; and then we made out to start it, and shifted it enough so the boat could go by. We didn't put it back again, as we would need the passage next day; whoever couldn't jump that ought to walk, we thought.

A little beyond there, the stream was fringed by undergrowth and saplings, and it was something like those pretty reaches we came through the day before; only here it was narrower, and we found it hard getting along.

We heard a cart rattling a little way off, and men talking; but we could see nothing of them. I thought they were loading hay How little they dreamed that a boat was moving along close by.

Soon after this, the branches began to grow across so thickly that it was terribly scratchy work, and at last we had to take the hatchet to them; it was the worst tangle we had come to. We hacked and pushed our way through this for a quarter of an hour, and made, may be, two or three dozen yards headway.

When the bushes thinned away, we found ourselves near the foot of a fall,— or more like rapids, —where the stream came down quite steeply for two or three rods, foaming and rushing over rocks; but fortunately there was a smooth grassy bank on the left, and we unloaded the boat and slid her up to where we could launch her above.

It seemed as though all the falling the water cared to do along here was done at this one place for now the current was quite gentle, so for a while

we had a pretty easy time;—and we weren't sorry,
I tell you; for our hewing, heaving and hauling had
made us very hot, as well as tired. Now we took
turns in towing along the bank; the steering was
so easy, it amounted to resting.

Our stream, the "Pequonset River," was now a
little less than twice the width of the boat, on an
average, and from one to two feet deep; it slid
quietly along, with a splash now and then as a frog
slung himself in the water before us.

THE OLD ORCHARD.

We passed an old orchard, where the trees were
all fringed with yellow-green lichens, and every one
had some dead branches; some were about all that
way. But a few old veterans were carrying brave
loads of apples, though I noticed there were no
windfalls on the ground;— which wasn't to be wondered at; for seven or eight half-grown pigs came
trotting up, and sniffed toward us with inquiring
grunts. Three of them escorted us a little way,

till I raised a splashing with the oar; then they showed us the graceful twist of their tails.

At last "Beames' Brook" came flowing in from the left with a swift current, pushing the boat over to the opposite bank. We thought it seemed to bring in about one-third of the water we had been traveling on; but there was enough yet in the main stream to float us, so the *Triton* was still pointed upward.

The bottom grew stony; once or twice a rock touched along underneath, then the boat bumped up on one and stuck. I got out—Joe was already out towing—but she wasn't very willing to come even then. There was more of a current; and, at last, it got to be such rugged traveling, that we said there wasn't any sense in grinding our boat to pieces (and fagging ourselves out) for the sake of getting her a quarter of a mile farther. So we didn't bother the *Triton* any longer, but left her at peace in a little pool at a bend, while we pushed on to do a little more exploring before sunset.

Once more the rushing of water grew louder as we advanced, but it was no mill-dam this time; the stream came foaming and leaping down a long, rocky slope, splitting and re-uniting, shooting over smooth inclines, tumbling off jutting shelves; it wasn't at rest a moment. The sound of a heavier plunge behind the trees came to us through the general uproar, and, in a few moments, we saw a double fall, which must have been nearly twenty feet high. At the top the stream divided, and poured down on each side upon a step a yard or two wide, where it united, and made the second plunge in one body down the middle.

This was the best fall we had come across; perhaps the one at the island, the first day, was as handsome in its way; but there was ten times as much water here.

Above, it still came rushing down the slope; at one place it had worn the rock in an odd fashion, making a narrow channel, or groove, a couple of yards long. Then we came to a sort of trough, large enough to hold three boats like ours, and three or four feet deep; here, at last, was a moment's halt in the dashing and foaming. We agreed that it was a capital bath-tub; but it was getting late, and we hadn't time to take advantage of it. From where the water spouted into its upstream end, we followed up the torrent for five minutes more, before coming to the level at the top, where it quieted down, and curved away into the woods at our left.

Here, on the top, it was clear of trees for quite a space, with rocks cropping out of the short turf all around.

"This hill must be the same as the one we rode up just before we came to the turnpike," said I. "This brook is a deal higher at Hollisville than at the Holcomb's."

To the right the ground rose to a small rocky ridge, and from there we could get a view in some directions. The spire of the "Orthodox" Church was in sight, about half a mile to the northwest. The sun was getting quite low; but the air was still unusually warm, without a breath of wind; to the north the clouds were piled in great "thunder-heads" of a deep pearl-gray, except where the edges to the west were touched with bright reddish-gold light. Suddenly a faint glimmer of lightning played beneath them, and was gone in an instant.

"Squally weather there!" said Joe. "If it travels down this way we'll find out how our tents'll shed rain!"

We thought we'd camp on a level spot across from the old orchard, and it was time to be getting back there. Our exploring had reached its limits. From this time we would be going back over the same ground (or water); but the fun wasn't over yet, and, as Joe said, it would be a deal easier now, with the current favoring us, the snags chopped away, and our dam built.

He said he wished we could take the latitude and longitude of this spot, as was the regular style with explorers, but I laughed at that. I said that as a degree of latitude was nearly seventy miles long, and one of longitude about fifty, at this distance from the equator, we hadn't counted much in that line, as yet. I didn't believe the Hollisville people troubled themselves much about their latitude and longitude.

We agreed, however, to raise a "cairn" of stones on the ledge, to mark our farthest point. This being duly done, we made our way past the falls and rapids to our boat.

"The *Triton's* farthest north!" exclaimed Joe.

"The head of navigation!" I echoed.

We towed her back to the meeting of the brook, then dropped easily down to the old orchard, where we hove the anchor ashore.

CHAPTER XXVIII.

Having reached our "Ultima Thule,"—if you know what that is— we were now ready for exploring of a humbler order; and the hope of coming across an apple of which we could endure a second bite drew us from one bent and gnarly tree to another, till we had wandered nearly across to the tumble-down fence at the upper end, where we found an ancient "July sweeting," which bore a few specimens which we thought worth pocketing, and there were just about enough to fill our pockets.

The pigs were nowhere to be seen; we concluded they had gone home for the night. There were a dozen or two bright yellow apples on a tree a few paces to the right, which looked as though they might be worth the trouble of sampling; but as we moved that way, we saw a chimney and a section of a weather-stained roof! I had felt that what we had taken was ours by right of discovery, and would otherwise go to waste, or at the best be crunched by hogs—but with a house close at hand, it seemed a little different. "Come on!" said Joe, "let's see what there is; if we pay for every apple on the place, it won't break us!"

On going through a bar-way, which had no bars, the

house stood in sight,—where the great bushes and wilderness of creepers running wild, would let it be seen, occasionally.

"It doesn't look very lively," said I.

"Nobody at home to-day, I should say!" remarked Joe.

But the door was wide open,—and most of the windows; to be sure, it was a hot day, but people don't generally smash out nine-tenths of the glass, even in the hottest weather, or punch out holes through the roof!

It was plain that nobody had lived there for a long time; the gray shingles on the roof and gables were curled by sun and gnawed by storm; around a great gap near one chimney were clustered the orange-red flowers of a huge trumpet-vine, which rose and spread at one side of the door, and was met from the other side by the sprays of a lilac-bush — or rather tree,— around whose stems clung long, thorny shoots of "high blackberry," with plenty of leaves and little fruit. The long grass, in what had been the path to the step, looked as though no one had disturbed it that summer; but Joe now proceeded to do so, observing, "This is an exploring expedition, I believe!"

After brushing and scratching through the bushes, we entered the doorway; the door, parted from its hinges, lay at one side. There was no "entryway"; we found ourselves at once in the kitchen,—

a good-sized room, half the lower story; the big joists above were planed smooth, and colored a dull black, as though from smoke, though perhaps they had been painted so.

There was a wainscot around two sides; on the other two it was mostly torn away, showing the studding timbers, which were hewn, not sawed, and showed the bark in some places; the spaces between were built up with small, rough stones, laid in mortar. Above the wainscot, where the plastering had come away in great patches, we could see that it had been spread on these stones, like a cellar wall; but it wasn't so altogether, for there were laths, too, in some places, and these were of various sizes; it was plain they had been split by hand. It seemed as though whoever did the work, couldn't make up his mind which was the least trouble,— to lay up the stones, or split and nail the laths; when he got tired of one, he changed to the other, for a rest. And the nails! no two alike, with big clumsy heads, and tough, slender shafts;— they were handmade, too.

"I wonder if they made their own hammers," said Joe, "or pounded these nails in with a stone!"

More than one-third of the floor boards were gone, leaving chasms,— which weren't deep, however, as there was no cellar under this half of the house. The fireplace was a big one, of course, and floored with large flat stones; we walked right in

"NOBODY AT HOME TO-DAY, I SHOULD SAY!" REMARKED JOE.

without stooping, and looked up the chimney at the sky. The chimney was built of stones, too — all sizes and kinds; on one side of it was a closet, with shelves still in place; on the other was a brick oven, with a small closet above, the door of which was gone. The windows were in various states; one hadn't even a sash, another had but one; and those with both had few whole panes; the glass was so crooked that it curled and twisted whatever was seen through it. The bushes and tall weeds grew up against the outside and shut out the light,— but more light would only have showed more plainly what a dismal, ruinous place it was.

In the eastern half were two rooms, about as dilapidated; each had a small fireplace across the inner corner, which opened into the same chimney. There was no hall; the stairs ran right up from the kitchen, and they looked so shaky we were almost afraid to try them. I was lighter, so I ventured up first.

It was a "story-and-a-half" house, and up stairs was a small room partitioned off over the southwest corner of the kitchen, and two at the other end, over the two down stairs. These rooms were lathed and plastered, leaving an unfinished garret in the middle and the northwest part.

Joe had now tip-toed up, and he called my attention to the top step, or landing, of the stairs; at one end, it was on the level of the garret floor, which had sagged down from that point, so the other end of the step, a yard away, stood at least three inches above the floor. "If the stairs hold their own as well as that, I guess we can trust 'em!" he said.

The partitions were built up with posts and slabs, most of which had plenty of the original bark still on ; against them the laths—or split sticks—were nailed. There were two good-sized holes in the roof, and the light poured in, and sifted through the cracks everywhere around ; if it hadn't been for that 'twould have been pretty dark, as the garret had only a little bit of a window in the gable.

The rooms weren't particularly interesting, except that the floors tipped every way, so it seemed pretty ticklish to walk on them ; the boards were gone in some places, and small holes stove through the ceilings of the rooms beneath, so we could look down in. Here were little fireplaces across the corners, just as below ; and an old rusty stove stood in front of one of them, the most modern thing in the place—unless a sparrow's nest, in the gap of the wall may have been of later date—and dozens of names penciled around on the plastering ; they were of all dates, from fifteen years back.

In the garret was what I knew for part of a spinning wheel, the legs and standards ; the wheel was gone. Joe set it under the break in the roof for him to perch on, while he reached out for some of the trumpet-flowers.

I noticed that the chimneys were built of stone up to just under the roof, and then the bricks began.

"Wonder if they made their own bricks!" said I.

"Perhaps they got them from that brick-yard down the river; that looks as though it might be about as old as this place. It had the monopoly then, most likely, and charged up good and solid; so the people here just economized on their bricks."

The sun had set while we were yet in the orchard, and it was time for us to be making our camp; so we went down stairs; we didn't slam down, three steps at a time, and a jump; but stepped quietly and politely, as though the minister had come to tea. Then it struck Joe we hadn't been down cellar. "Let's do the whole thing, it'll only take a minute more."

The ricketty stairs were still in place, with two steps gone at the bottom; and on the wall above, the fading light streamed in through the sashless window, showing in big, straggling letters:

> Ye who come here for sport or fun
> Ye gidy things be carefull how you run
> For in the celler right down here
> There lies the murderd Peter Greer.

Joe looked at me, and we both laughed. "If he's dead, he won't hinder us!" said he, and started down; and I followed.

I knew that ridiculous stuff had been written

by some young idiot who didn't know how to spell; but it made the place seem different, somehow.

Joe jumped to the bottom, and so did I; but before I touched ground there were wild ejaculations behind us! and a thumping and rushing which unsettled me so that I came down on all-fours. 'Twas three of those miserable hogs, and they scuttled out through a gap in the wall; I saw what it was in less than a second but it took a minute or two for me to get over the first part of that second. I didn't let Joe know that; we both laughed, and he said the "murderd" Peter seemed to have plenty of society; if he'd known he was receiving company, he wouldn't have intruded.

But we didn't find anything there worth staying for, and in two minutes more we were outside, taking our last look at the desolate old shanty, with the vines clambering and flowers blooming over its old mossy roof, humped like the back of a dromedary.

CHAPTER XXIX.

We hurried through the orchard, and were soon busy with our camp, which was on the east side of the river, thus setting bounds to the inquisitive snouts of the porkers, in case they should be the earlier risers. I was taking the sail off the mast, that it might serve as my tent once more, when Joe exclaimed, "Gracious! those fish! we mustn't forget *them!*"

Sure enough! but we weren't hungry enough to care about cooking them, especially when it was so warm; and as they weren't fresh-caught now, anyway, we thought we would try and keep them over night. They were in the stern locker; it wasn't a refrigerator, exactly, this weather, and they were rather dry and dull-looking; but a rinsing freshened them up some.

Joe thought he'd put them in the brook, as the coolest place, and began stringing them together; but I feared the pigs might swim across after them. Joe didn't believe they liked swimming enough for that; but he admitted that a dog or something might happen along, and 'twas best to be on the safe side; so we dug out a little basin in the shore, close to the water, which ran in by a short channel we made; when the hollow was full, and had settled clear, Joe laid in the fish, and covered the place with a big flat stone; we set a few more heavy stones close around, to fortify against rooting. "We don't want to lose that pickerel!" said Joe.

It didn't take ten minutes to get our tents all rigged; we'd grown pretty expert by this time.

"Does it seem possible, Joe, that we were in this boat at Pierhaven only day before yesterday?"

"Or that we slept in a regular bed the night before! Well; I wouldn't mind keeping this up for three or four weeks!"

"Provided we had good weather."

"Oh, well, explorers aren't fit for much who can't stand a little weather. We're not made of sugar or salt, and a shower or two won't melt us!"

Which was so, no doubt; still I think neither Joe nor I was anxious to be put to the test.

We walked up the gentle easterly slope to the top of a knoll, on which were a few tall chestnut trees. From here we could see the deserted house, with the pale light from the west touching its crumbling chimneys, and showing dimly the roof of another building, — a barn, probably — not far off; we hadn't perceived it when we were near by.

The heavy clouds still hung in the north and east, a dusky, leaden mass. Suddenly the lightning flickered from deep within their midst, showing a beautiful maze of light and dark cloud shapes piled above each other, and reaching miles back to the horizon; the next instant the display had vanished like magic, and the place where it had been was again flat and murky as a fog-bank. In half a minute, another space farther around to the east flashed out into glowing heights and gloomy depths, stretching away like a range of enchanted mountains, — and then left us to imagine that wide and rugged region in the bit of dull gray cloud that took its place.

These two storm-centers kept answering each other, and were echoed by fainter glimmers between.

"This is something like your moon-cloud you were talking about,—showing up bright as day in the night-time. Maybe it'll work 'round by-and-by, and give you a chance to see how it looks close to."

"Let her come!" I answered, "the old *Triton's* sail'll be over by that time. I'd a deal rather it would rain to-night, if its got to, and be over by morning. We'll camp to-morrow night,—where?"

"Let's see," said Joe. "We'll go back with the current, faster than we came; and we won't have to stop and build a dam, or drive to Hollisville again, though those Holcomb boys will want to talk with us awhile, I suppose. Now, last night we camped a little this side of Harlow's Pond; and to-morrow we ought to get farther down than that."

"We ought to get considerably farther down. You remember that hard place, where we first had to shove through the branches,—that's just below

Shad Factory; and then come those pretty reaches where the trees arch over. There isn't a crack you could throw a dog through, all along. The first place I can think of where we could find room for the tents, is where that beech tree grows across."

"Well, that's a good place; if we can't go farther before dark, we'll stop there."

The night-hawks were sailing and plunging far above; their constant squeaking came down to us, and every few seconds one of them would give a dive, then turn quickly up; and we could hear the strange booming they make at such times.

"I remember the first time I ever noticed those chaps," said Joe. "I was at uncle Townley's, in Connecticut,— I couldn't have been more than five years old,— and I was sitting with him on the steps, about this time of day. I heard these birds keeping up their noise, and watched their capers; uncle told me they were 'night-hawks,' and said they were calling 'beef! beef! beef!' and then they roared out 'pork!' when they came swooping down.

"He didn't tell me they were little harmless creatures, not as big as a pigeon, and lived on mosquitoes and such things;— and he never dreamed that for years afterward my idea was that they were great, black, ferocious fellows, as large as I, or pretty nearly so, which hankered after beef-and-pork as a general thing, but were willing perhaps to try small boy, if nothing else was handy. I didn't fancy night-hawks for quite a while; there was something dreadful about the very name of 'em, and when I heard them screaming savagely for their 'beef-and-pork!' I didn't want to be too far from cover."

"It does beat all what notions little fellows get hold of, doesn't it? Now there's any quantity of boys,— big ones, too,— who'd rather face a hornet any time than a dragon-fly.'

"I know it; I used to believe myself that they'd

sew my mouth up, if they took a fancy to; I'm sure I don't know what I thought *I'd* be doing while they were at it! To-day even, I've dodged two or three times, before I thought, when one came whizzing closer than common. I think it was seeing you handle one, two or three years ago, that got me over that fancy."

"Well, that ought to offset that scorpion business you were so tickled about yesterday, seems to me."

He was good-natured enough to admit this; and shortly afterward we went down to camp, and turned in.

Some time in the night I got to dreaming about being with Joe in that tumble-down house; I don't remember anything plain about it, except that it was rather dismal and "scary," and that, finally, Joe persisted in climbing out on the roof through the gap. I didn't want him to, for I was certain 'twouldn't hold; and sure enough! about half the roof came smashing down, letting in a great glare of light, and he slammed and crashed through the floor into the lower story. It was terrific! and, just as I made up my mind he was killed, I felt myself waking up.

I knew where I was, right off; and was glad enough to know it, though I felt pretty well "jolted," same as I did when we met the pigs down cellar. The night was dark as pitch, but it wasn't still; I heard a patter and rush; I put up my hand to feel of the tent, and found it was wet.

Then I knew it was raining, but I didn't mind; that made it all the cosier. I turned over, and was thinking in a sleepy sort of way how those rain-drops started from away up, a mile or two, may be, aiming right for my face; and the stanch little sail stopped 'em at the last moment,— when there came a blaze of lightning and a crash and roll of thunder that started me wider awake than ever. I lay waiting for another, but it seemed a long time before it came, and then it didn't amount to nearly as much as the first, — and so the storm tapered off by degrees, with glimmerings and mutterings farther and farther off. I guess I was asleep before it quite got through.

Next morning, the first thing I was aware of was the same pattering on the cloth roof just above my head,— so we would have to make our downward start in the rain, after all. It seemed to me that the boat had a slight tilt, or "list," to port. As I got wider awake, I raised my head to get what view of things outside the tent-opening might allow, and found I was looking nearly down-stream; whereas the last twilight of the evening before had shown me the crooked interlacing-branches of the old apple-trees above the opposite bank!

This startled me, and I scrambled up and put out my head; then I saw that the stream had swelled enough to throw the boat around sideways. I had kept up the practice of knotting the painter to the cot-stake, so there had been no drifting. The water had plainly been higher than now, as the *Triton* was aground on the sloping shore, with the edge of the current washing along her port side.

It wasn't raining very hard now; still I thought fit to try to dress inside the tent. It wasn't as high as the other, or "shore" tent; and *that* wasn't any *too* high, though when you were lying down, 'twas all right. I found it a wofully awkward job; my shoulders would rub up against the cold, wet slope on either side, spite of all I could do; but after protracted misery I finally pulled on my waterproof, and crawled out to take observations.

Joe didn't seem to be awake, yet, I wondered what time it could be; my dial wouldn't work this morning. The wind was coming in puffs, from the southeast; everything was dripping, and I didn't see much chance of making a fire; still I didn't know as there was any need of one, after all. Yes there was, though—those fish! If they weren't attended to they would spoil, and that couldn't be thought of, when they were our own catching, and we had carried them so far.

Perhaps the lamp in our lantern,—which we hadn't used yet—might heat a tin plate enough to fry them.

"Hullo!" hailed Joe, "seems to me your tent looks rather lopsided! You see now I wasn't such a fool when I talked about freshets the other evening. If you hadn't hitched to this stake, you'd have been snaked down the chute of rocks below here; and I'd have had to get the Holcombs to drag Glenn's Pond for you!" "Not much!" I returned. "I'd have stuck to the *Triton* every time, you can be sure!"

"If you had, you'd kerwholloped over the dam, for Mr. Odell to gather up in detachments!"

"Well," I laughed, "that's no worse than I really thought had happened to you, for a little while!" And then I told him my dream.

"'Twas one of those thunder-claps did that for you!" said he. "Must have made a strong impression; I see you're in mourning yet!" (My waterproof was black, of course.) "If you were awake," he went on, "why didn't you answer when I yelled?"

"I didn't hear you; it must have been before I woke up."

"Well, I guess the first of it roused me. After it had been flashing and whanging a quarter of an hour, I judged you couldn't be asleep through *that*, so I tried to start a conversation; but you never made a sign, — and I made up my mind that if the 'thunder-drum of heaven' couldn't start you, 'twas no use for *me* to try."

In a few moments more, Joe was dressed; and I got him his water-proof from the locker.

"The first thing, now, is to cook those fish."

"Just what I was thinking of; but every particle of wood 'round here is soaked."

"Not all I guess. I saw lots of it under cover, in various assorted sizes, yesterday,— up that way," pointing through the orchard.

The old house! why hadn't I thought of it!

"But where are the fish? It can't be that the river has washed away those stones— Ho! they're under the boat!"

We laid hold of the *Triton*, and hauled her farther ashore; and where she had been were the stones, as we had left them the night before; and the fish were there too, all right.

"Those fish were well guarded!" said I. "Nobody could have taken them without passing over my dead body!"

"Your sound-asleep body, you mean! 'Twouldn't have been anything great to have got 'em, the way you slept through that storm. Now we'll go right up and start the fire."

We thought we might as well take the wet tents, to see if we could dry them before folding them away; and the blankets, too, which were pretty damp, especially Joe's; he said the rain trickled from the tent to the edge of the cot, in some places, and soaked around underneath.

So we struck camp; we drove a stake on the orchard side, and tied the boat to it. It was still raining, and we hoisted the umbrella to shelter the blankets, while we made our way to the house.

CHAPTER XXX.

The old house looked more forlorn than ever; black and sodden, with all the bushes and weeds wet and dripping; but it was scarcely as wet inside as might have been expected, considering how far the ramshackle old concern was from being weather-tight.

We had brought the hatchet, of course, and while Joe cleaned the fish I knocked off a number of the laths, and hacked up two of the floor-boards that hadn't caught much of the drip.

Then I piled the driest sticks under the great chimney, and struck a match.

"Little this fireplace knew about matches when they started the first fire in it, or for some time after, likely," I remarked. "Fancy getting down here of a morning, with the mercury shrunk 'way down below freezo, to find every spark out, and then having to rasp away for ten minutes or so with flint and steel!"

"Little it knew about kerosene, either!"

"No; that came in use a good while after matches. Perhaps people got through living here before it was used at all."

Our fire looked pretty small in that big chimney, but it was equal to frying the fish, and they did beautifully. While Joe was attending to that I extracted a few of the ancient nails, and, with them and some cord I had, I hung the tent and sail so they could drip and dry as much as they would; then I stretched up the blankets in front of the fireplace.

There was nothing to sit down on, but that didn't trouble us long. I knocked a couple of flat stones out of the front corner of the chimney, where they had been laid in together a little more than a foot above the hearth. One end of one of the floor-boards was wedged into this place, and the other was propped on the remnant of the spinning-wheel, which I brought down from above; and there was a bench that would hold us, and three or four more, if they'd been there.

I don't believe a breakfast was ever more enjoyed in that old kitchen. We had fish, doughnuts, cheese, crackers and huckleberry pie; and might have had eggs, if we'd wanted. It's pretty certain the folks who used to live there would have been surprised if they could have foreseen that breakfast, and taken in the whole look of the place, with our tents and blankets strung about,—part of the floor ripped up to do the cooking and another part to sit down on. And of all the places where we had breakfasted since we stowed away Peggy's flapjacks, this was the queerest, though it was in a house and the others were out-doors.

After the fish were cooked, we had piled on the rest of the wood and it blazed finely while we were eating, so the blankets steamed, and we edged to the farther end of our bench; the place didn't seem nearly as dismal as at first. We heard some friends of the ill-fated Peter, down below, after a while; but this time our blood didn't freeze worth a cent. Perhaps they'd got some notion that eating was going on, and were willing to help.

We didn't hurry with our breakfast, for there was nothing very inspiring in the idea of cruising in rainy weather! and when we did get up, and begin to rearrange our bags, and feel of the blankets to see how they were drying, the rain suddenly set in heavier than ever. It had been growing dark the last few minutes; but we hadn't thought much of it. So we waited for the shower to let up, before starting.

In a minute, the slow drip-drip from a dozen or two places overhead, turned to little jets and streamlets, which spattered on our bench, and all around. We rushed for our waterproofs, which I had hung on some nails that stood out already for them in the closet; but they were uncomfortable to sit in, and another bright idea popped into Joe's head. He said we could spread the waterproofs on the floor above, and then sit at our ease.

Well, we carried it out; — partly for the fun of the thing, for it did seem ridiculous to have to cover the garret floor, to keep from being wet through in the kitchen and I made the thing more harmonious by speading my umbrella while we were attending to it,—and there was reason, too; for the water just poured through the roof-cracks. I pointed out to Joe the place where I dreamed he smashed through.

"I'm glad it isn't so," said I, "for you carried away pretty nearly all this side of the roof."

He guessed I'd have had a worse dream than that, if I'd been washed down-stream,—but I don't know. The lively part then would have come after waking up.

Our bench, and the region around it in front of the fireplace, was now free from drip, and we sat down to wait events. The water ran down the side of the chimney in quite a little stream, and soaked in between the hearth-stones; it didn't drop into the fire much, as the wind gave it a slant; but we poked the embers a little nearer the front, and laid on what fragments of wood were within reach ; we didn't need it to keep us warm, but it looked pleasant, and drove off the damp feeling.

The down-pour slackened up, and the sky grew lighter; but there was still quite a patter.

"This is a south-easter!" said Joe. "'Open and shet's a sign of wet';—and there'll be such showers every few minutes, for may be half a day yet. We're more comfortable here, than we'd be brushing through the dripping trees, with the boat all wet, and having to bail her out every quarter of an hour. I move we wait till we're pretty sure the rain's over."

'Twas well enough we did; for soon it darkened up again, so the fire shed quite a bright, cheerful light around; then the clouds let loose once more, —not as hard, perhaps, but it lasted longer, so our wood was about used up. As soon as that shower held up, we went into the east rooms with the hatchet, and hacked and ripped away at the dry places till we had enough to fill the fireplace "chock up," if we'd put it all in at once.

"We're the last people to live here," said Joe, "and we'll work the old place for all it's worth."

It must have been a deal more trouble to build that house, than it would be to put up one like it now; and I wonder how they'd have felt when they were laying that chimney, if they'd been told that the timbers and laths which were hewed and split with so such labor, would be broken up to make a fire in it. But all houses must end in some way; and this was better than to burn up without doing anybody any good, the way most do.

"Let's play tens," said Joe, taking out his knife, and opening it half-way.

In case you've never played it, I'll just say that you give your knife a little pitch in the air, so it'll whirl once or twice, and come down with the point sticking in the board or log you're sitting on. If it comes down on the handle, or in some way so it falls over without sticking, the other fellow takes his turn. If the point sticks in, with the end of the handle touching the board, that's ten; if it sticks with the handle in the air, you count as many tens as you can get fingers between it and the board;— and in either case you keep up your play, till you let the knife fall over. The "game" is generally a thousand.

There's a throw which is sometimes allowed to count for a hundred,—when the knife happens to lie on the back of the handle without falling over, but that depends on the build of the knife; sometimes it comes that way so often it wouldn't be fair to count it.

It's a game I don't think much of, any more than marbles; it seems too still and poky for an out-door play; but this was just the time and place for it. So we took our places on a soft board, and Joe gave the first toss. We each took several turns before anything was counted; and even when we had "got the hang" we didn't seem to get along very fast; for though it was a big, heavy knife, he'd cut out so many fish-fins with it lately that it was hard for it to stick even in a half-rotten old board like this. So after the first game, we took mine, and then it was more interesting. We counted the "hundred" throw, with Joe's knife,— anything to get ahead; — but with mine we had to give that up; for Joe got so he could make it about once in three times.

We played six games, and Joe beat in four; by that time it seemed more like clearing up than it had yet; so we folded the blankets, which had lost the greater part of their moisture, and the tent and sail, which still held a pretty good share; to be sure, they had more to start with. But the weather shifted so quickly, that by the time we were ready to start, the sun had given up all idea of breaking through;— and we heard a low bellow of thunder, which didn't seem intended to invite us forth.

So we waited a bit, to see what it did mean; and soon another showed that it was coming our way. "We'll let that beast get by!" said Joe.

We put down the things, and settled on our bench;— and before the next peal came a glimmer of lightning. Then I remembered having read somewhere that you can tell the distance of lightning by counting the seconds between the flash and the thunder.

I mentioned this to Joe, who straightway got out his Waterbury, and held it all ready; while I fingered my pulse, which I knew averaged a little faster than once a second, — about seventy-five a minute. With the next flash we began counting; and just as I came to eight, the rumbling began. Joe called out "seven!" But the loudest of it came a moment later; and then it growled itself away by degrees into nothing.

"Where do you stop, — the beginning, or the biggest crack?" inquired Joe.

I said the beginning came from the nearest point of the flash, and that was what we cared about. Then I calculated: sound travels about twelve hundred feet a second, I remembered (1090 feet with the air at the freezing point); 1200 times 8 are 9600. Here came another flash, but it was feebler, and I didn't stop to count, — a mile is 5280 feet;— 'twas nearly two miles off.

Then there was a pretty sharp flash, with a rattling peal, — scarcely three seconds after, Joe said. That was within a mile. The storm was right on the road for us; now the rain began to come down heavily.

The next gleam was dazzling, and a tremendous crash followed right after it, so that Joe admitted that it was shorter than his watch would note; and

I shouldn't wonder if my pulse beat too quick time for close reckoning for a few moments after that crack. The rain kept pouring in fine style for some time, but there were only three or four more claps, and these not so near.

CHAPTER XXXI.

Joe said it reminded him of a time when he went fishing in Connecticut, two summers before. He and his two cousins, Dave and Fred, went about two miles, to "Spectacle Pond," as it was called. It was something like Glenn's Pond, only more so, for the narrow part of it was a mere creek, about an eighth of a mile long. It was like two ponds strung together. They started after dinner, to make an afternoon of it.

"They let me have the biggest rod,—'twas a bamboo pole, near twenty feet long. That was very polite of them, I knew; but after a while I didn't appreciate it so much. The fish weren't biting lively, by any means, and it got to be tedious business holding that pole straight out, for we hadn't any boat, but stood on the bank and reached as far as we could, to get our hooks into deep water.

"Well, that pole grew heavier than you'd think — it seemed light as could be when I began, — so I let the end down in the water; it was hollow, you know, and buoyed up first-rate, and that was nice and easy for a time. They told me, though, 'twouldn't pay; the bamboo would soak like a sponge, and so it did; when I lifted it out it was a deal worse than before. So after a little while I let it slump in again.

"I'd only caught one fish, a shiner; the others had three or four apiece; they were more used to that sort of fishing. When I tried to hold out my pole again it was 'most as heavy as our mast. I saw it

wouldn't do to let that go on, so I knocked off awhile; and set to building a little wharf of stones and sand, so I could reach farther out. We didn't like to stand in the water, for they said there were 'bloodsuckers' (leeches) in the pond.

"In time the fish seemed to find out there was something going on over our way, and began coming around to see about it; at any rate the boys were hauling them in faster, and I thought I would try my luck again. But I had to groan when I felt the heft of the pole; and Dave,—he was a stout fellow, a year older than I,—was good-natured enough to offer to change with me.

"His pole was all right as to weight, but it had been broken off near the middle, and spliced together again with five or six yards of fish-line wound around. But of course I didn't care for looks, and soon I hauled in a bull-pout, and kept on till I had four, besides a perch and the shiner.

"By this time, we'd been there about two hours; it was hot and still, same as yesterday afternoon. There were high trees most of the way around the pond, so we couldn't see the sky down toward the horizon, except out east, where the water stretched away; so we didn't notice the clouds creeping up but all at once the sun stopped shining, and we heard the thunder muttering, 'way off.

"I heard it coming nearer, and thought 'twas time for us to start, but the others were having good fun, and the afternoon was hardly half over. They wanted to get good big strings, Fred especially; he said we needn't mind a little sprinkling, we could run 'tween the drops, if it came our way, and he didn't believe it would. I saw he didn't want to believe it, anyway.

"Well, the thunder grew louder and louder, and the lightning began to show up; so finally they were ready to leave. The way home led across lots, through some woods and across lots again, without a house anywhere near, for the first mile. We hadn't got far when the rain began to patter down in great drops, and Fred wanted us to run for a big oak at the edge of the pasture, and take shelter under it; but just then there crinkled down a savage-looking streak of chain-lightning,— we all saw it; and a terrific clap followed, next moment, that made us feel rather shaky.

"Then I told them, it had been observed and put on record, that oak trees had been struck oftener than all other kinds together; and it was dangerous to be near any kind of tree in a thunder-storm. So we gave a wide berth to the oak.

"Now the rain poured down in torrents; we ran, as a matter of course, though we might just as well have taken it easy. Talk about running 'tween the drops! we hit enough of 'em to do for us; in three minutes we couldn't be wetter.

"A little house showed suddenly through the thick rain, a few yards ahead, but we didn't think of trying to get under cover there. 'Twas a powder-house, where they stored powder, a long way from where it would be likely to do any harm if it went off; we had passed near by it, coming out, and Dave had told me about it, and how there was ten thousand pounds of powder in there — so he said — that belonged to the militia. And now, as we caught sight of it, another streak had to tear down with a crash fit to take your head off, and we didn't know at first but the plaguy thing had "busted"; it couldn't have made much more racket. So we dodged one side and made a curve to the left, in case the next bolt should touch her off.

"Then we came to the little patch of woods, with a narrow path winding through it. I had scared them about trees; so when there pealed out another ripper just as we were going in, Dave sung out 'Now let's clip it through these woods like everything!' and tore ahead like mad, with Fred after him.

"I was about winded; and just then there came something else into my head, that I had heard or read of,— it seemed as though I knew too much, or not enough, I couldn't make out which,— only there was no being safe, any thing you might do. What I thought of was, that a body moving rapidly is more likely to get struck, because the air is a little thinner just behind,— in the wake, you might say,— and the lightning takes the easiest path, and follows it right up. I think that's only a notion, that's never been proved; for I never heard of a railway train being struck, and that ought to stand as a good chance as anything.

"Anyway, I tried to yell it to Dave; but I was too much out of breath, and they were plunging along ten rods ahead. I tagged after, trying to keep them in sight and to steer my rod clear of obstacles, as the path turned;— in a minute I ran it against a tree, lance fashion, and broke it short off three or four feet from the tip; it was wound with line, as I said, which went beyond the break, and was finally tied fast about the middle of the piece and that came off. So that just unwound; and the thing dragged and skipped crossways in the rear, catching first one end, then the other; but I held with a desperate grip to the main part of the rod, and the line didn't give way.

"I dragged anchor through the last third of the woods, and came up with the others where they were walking along beyond; at last they saw no use in running any longer. We had to laugh when we looked at each other; our clothes hung like bathing suits; the brim of Dave's old felt hat was beaten down, and all our hats were dripping like umbrellas; if anybody ever looked like drowned rats, we did then. The field was covered an inch or two with water that hadn't had time to soak in; it was like that place where we hauled the boat through the grass, and we splashed along in it the same way. We said it wouldn't do to let our fish drop, for they could swim right off;— and I remember thinking with a sort of envy that the fish in the pond didn't mind the storm a bit — 'twas all the same to them.

"Neither did the people in the house we now saw ahead; and we'd have been glad enough to make for it if the rain had just started; but as it was, the storm was beginning to let up; and we sneaked around back to that house, out of sight, and came into the road a good ways below. Dave and Fred knew the fellows there, and didn't want to hear any remarks!"

"What'd they say, when you got home?"

"O, Aunt Townley was pretty mad when she saw us, and said we'd got to go to bed right off, and stay there — so we did, and had a jolly time whanging each other with pillows. It turned out that Uncle saw us from the window of the barn, where he was sharpening tools, and had a good laugh over the figure we cut; perhaps he spoke a good word for us; anyhow they let us get up in an hour or so, and Fred lent me his best suit. We cleaned our fish, and had 'em for supper; and they were good; they'd had no chance to get dry, like those we had this morning."

CHAPTER XXXII.

All at once something came tumbling down the chimney into the fire. We weren't looking, and it startled us a little when it lit among the embers, and set the sparks flying.

It looked like a good-sized lump of dirt; but when we picked it up, we saw it was a nest — a chimney-swallow's nest — of sticks and grass stuck together with a kind of glue. It had been fastened to the stones inside, up toward the top; and the water running down had washed it loose. 'Twas lucky for the swallows that their family had been raised, and taken wing; if it had been spring-time, there'd have been "dropped eggs" for us, only it wouldn't have been easy to dish them up.

I had noticed quite a bunch at the side of the chimney, when we had looked up the evening before; but thought it was one of the stones. I looked again now, and it was gone. It seemed to us a queer place to live; perhaps the warm draught was what they liked, but with it they had to stand the smoke — still, there's nothing like being brought up to a thing, and perhaps when they first flew out, they thought the air outside was too fresh, and needed seasoning.

Joe spoke of the barn we had seen the evening

before, and said it would be a shame not to explore that too, when we were sitting around close by, doing nothing. So we set out with the umbrella — for the waterproofs were needed to keep the house dry — and when shortly the barn came in sight, it didn't look so ruined and forsaken as the house, by considerable. You don't expect so much of a barn, though; if there's no paint, and not much in the way of windows, you're not surprised; and you don't mind if there's nobody to answer the bell.

But here there wasn't even a door; and though there were no big breaks in the roof, 'twas like a starlit sky, when we went in and looked up. Four stalls stood across one end; they were occupied, not by cows or horses, but by half a dozen pigs, who looked interested and said good-day, but didn't seem at all afraid. They were beginning to feel acquainted, I suppose. There was a floor under the stalls, which reached across in front of the door; the rest was bare ground, and above on that side was a hay-loft, with a few boards left, stretching across.

It didn't take long to see all there was; and we made up our minds the house was more comfortable, as we could have a fire there; so we left the pigs in undisturbed possession, carrying away two or three loose boards to split up.

The rain still pattered down, and there was no prospect of any change at present. We overhauled our accounts,— Joe had paid for some butter and brown bread, and I had paid for the things at Hollisville; and now we squared up. We went up stairs and pored over the names written around, but found none we knew except those of the Holcomb boys. Ben's was scrawled in three different

places. There were faces, too; may be the writers meant them for their own portraits, but it's to be hoped that nobody who ever lived looked like them.

There was a vacant space of plaster in the northeast room, nearly a yard square, and we put down our names and the date in elegant style as time was no object just then. Joe was famous among the boys for the way he could print in "Old English"; and he drew up a grand inscription, with scrolls and flourishes all around, and took up the whole space, and made all the other scribblings look pretty cheap, I tell you. It read this way, starting right under our names:

> Commanders
>
> of the
>
> Triton Exploring Expedition,
>
> The First within the Memory of Man
>
> to Reach this Point
>
> from the Sea by Water.

It looked very imposing; but, as like as not, whoever saw it afterward took it for a piece of vaporing instead of solid fact.

Joe came across an old pair of trowsers, in a dark corner, and poked them out into the light "to see if they belonged to the first settler," he said. "Perhaps the cloth was spun on that identical wheel!"

But I didn't think it likely they spun fancy cassimeres on it; the first settler, too, would have worn "knee-breeches"; and though these were well fringed around the bottom, and would have been knee-breeches in a little longer wearing, they plainly began their career as "long trowsers," and finished it, as like as not, on some tramp of the present day. So he kicked them back into the corner.

We had risen later than usual that morning, and it was now past noon; so we had dinner, the principal dish being the pickerel, reserved from breakfast. We used some of the milk in making a cup apiece of hot chocolate, and it was good, you may believe.

Then we got so tired of being penned up, that we about made up our minds to start in the rain, after all. Joe said it was the wettest rain he ever saw,— "except that one at Spectacle Pond," I suggested.

"Yes, but there was some let up to that. This comes down as easy as though it had just started; it seems to think itself the regular and only thing, like the rainy season in the tropics. I guess that moon we saw the other night meant something, after all!"

But we hadn't seen the worst of it, yet; it came on a few minutes afterward. First it began to thunder and lighten again, and before long it was flashing and banging away at a pretty good rate. We went up stairs, where we could look out toward the southeast, and saw the rain coming in a solid sheet, shutting out one range of trees after another;

soon it began streaming so fast through the roof cracks that we were driven down stairs again.

It was dark enough down there then; but in a few seconds came a glare that seemed to blaze all over the room, and almost before we could wink, the thunder went off like a cannon. It fairly stunned us, and I thought for a moment that it had demolished the old bungalow, and us with it.

It didn't take long, of course, for us to find out that we still held together; but by the way the water streamed down into the room, it seemed as though what was left of the roof must have been carried away. The waterproofs still kept their place, though, and sheltered the space beneath.

"We're safe now!" declared Joe; "if it didn't strike here, it must have close by, and it won't come so near again."

It stayed 'round that neighborhood for quite a while, however, and there were two or three splitting cracks;—but the way the rain kept up was what surprised us—the same tremendous pour, right along. We heard complaints from the pigs, down cellar, and judged it was getting too deep for them; but there was plenty of room outside where they could still touch bottom, and a washing would do them no harm, anyway.

"Joe, this'll fill our boat!"

"That's so—but there isn't much inside; the oars and spars, and the tent-stakes; but water won't hurt them."

"No; but we don't want them to float out and away, and there's the lantern and feeder in the locker,— still, that doesn't matter much; but what bothers me is, that the river's filling up, too. If there's much of a current, it may carry her down."

He didn't believe that could be; for not only was she fastened to the stake, but the grapnel was up ashore, with the flukes well planted. But we both felt rather anxious; and when in about half an hour the rain suddenly seemed exhausted, and stopped almost altogether, we went up-stairs for our waterproofs. It was as wet up there as though there hadn't been any roof at all; still there was as much as before, for all we could see, and it was pretty certain the lightning hadn't touched it.

"It's because there ain't any lightning-rods," asserted Joe; "that's what saved it!"

There had been three houses struck, near Pierhaven, in the last two years;— one in February!— and they all had lightning-rods, but Uncle Andrew said they weren't fixed right. He said that good-sized copper-rods, well insulated, and leading off to running water, would be good protection;—but you don't often find them that way.

CHAPTER XXXIII.

We started out; and now it seemed less rainy outside than in, with the water dripping from the ceiling all around. We walked rapidly down through the orchard, and when we came in sight of the stream, how wide it was! away up over the bank, with a swift muddy current;—and no sign of the boat to be seen!

We were frightened then, and no mistake; if the *Triton* should go over the dam at Odell's, that would be "the last of her," as Tom had said of his boat. Besides there was that short piece of rapids not far below, where the water rushed down over the rocks.

We followed along as near as we could, though in some places the water ponded away out over the meadows; still the trees were not thick, and we could have seen the boat if she had drifted ashore anywhere.

At the rapids the stream wasn't so much wider than usual, for there was a little valley here, with high banks; but it was filled so full we wouldn't have known there were any rocks there, if we hadn't seen them the day before; the turbid water leaped down in big smooth rollers, without foaming, till it reached the bottom. To think that the *Triton* had plunged down that torrent! But, as Joe said, there was a deep pool at the foot, and if she'd got through without touching the rocks, as was likely, she wouldn't be hurt. And the boy's dam wasn't much to be dreaded, — but the one at Odell's was quite another matter; a sheer plunge of twenty feet to the stones below.

"Perhaps the Holcombs have caught her," I ventured; "they must be out watching their dam."

"I hope she hasn't smashed into their water-wheel!" rejoined Joe. "That'd finish up both concerns, in a hurry!"

When we reached the woods, we had a hard time of it for a while. The stream was several yards wide; in some places you couldn't tell how wide it was, or where the middle was, for it flowed all around among the tree-trunks; but we felt bound to see every foot, for she'd stop along here, if anywhere. We waded out into the water, pushing aside the wet boughs and peering here and there, and several times we climbed up among the slippery branches and dripping leaves, to get a better view. Now and then we saw where we had hacked our way the day before, and those places showed us where the channel went.

We spent upward of an hour in this disheartening way, without seeing anything of the *Triton*. We thought we must be nearly down to the stepping-stones, and below them there was nothing to stop her, unless the water-wheel, as Joe had suggested. We were feeling pretty blue. This kind of exploring — in search of our boat, instead of in it — didn't suit our ideas at all, and I began to think how it would seem to explore down below for her fragments, — a thwart here, a piece of the gunwale there.

We were wet to our waists, and nearly tired out. I had about given up hope, when I saw a piece of rope waving in the water, then one of the tent-stakes to which it was fastened, caught across a couple of trees growing close together. I waded in and found the other stake floating, still fast to the other end.

I don't know as there was any great comfort in this, still it put a little more interest into the search; and I was just going to call out to Joe, who was some little distance farther down, but he got ahead of me. "Here she is! hurrah! here she is, all right!" I heard him shout; and perhaps I didn't rush!

There she was, a little to one side of the channel, where it made a sudden turn; but the stream now disregarded the curve, and washed right ahead over the bank. She was tilted up sideways against a tree, with another trunk bracing the stern, so the current held her fast; the water around her was nearly a foot deep, and must have been higher still, to have put her there, and then let one side down.

We examined her carefully, and she seemed to be sound, except for several "dents" and rubbed places; we couldn't tell, yet, whether she was strained enough to leak. Two of the three oars were still aboard; we had stowed them in the bottom, and the "fore-peak" and after-thwart had held them from floating out; the short steering-oar was gone, however, and so were the mast and sprit, the cot-stakes and bailing-pan; but we scarcely thought of them, overjoyed as we were to find our boat safe and whole. In the locker were the lantern and oil-can, our extra rope and cord, nails, etc., and the fish-lines; all thoroughly wet, of course, but that wouldn't hurt them.

It was out of the question to take her back to the orchard, against the current there was running; and we were at first uncertain what to do next. We thought of launching her into the channel and going farther down to where we could haul her out on the meadows, but then we would have to carry our bags, blankets, etc., some distance farther before we could put them aboard,— unless, indeed, we went back for them at once, and then went down with the boat and made a camp somewhere below.

Joe was for doing this; but I argued that we were wet already, and it would be hard to keep our blankets dry while coming down through the woods, or indeed afterward, the boat being all wet inside; and the rain was still pattering on the leaves, with no sign of clearing up. There was no sense in being damp and chilly all night, when we could sit by the fire that evening at the house, and sling our cots from the ceiling.

Joe didn't like the idea of sleeping in that ruined, dismal place, instead of our cosy little tents; and neither did I, for that matter; but he admitted that it was the least of the two evils, and that wet blankets, might prove to be anything but cheerful.

The next thing was to put the *Triton* in as good shape as we could. We righted her, and towed her farther in among the trees; it was then we found the anchor-rope had parted. That must have been done at the rapids; if it had caught anywhere else, it would have held her, we thought. The painter hadn't parted, but the stake had pulled right up, and was still fast at the end; I had driven that stake pretty firmly, I thought, but very likely the earth was washed away from around it.

If we pulled her too far in, it would be more work to get her into the stream, next morning; still we wanted her to be out of the current, in case of another freshet. We stopped at a place about ten yards from where we found her; the water there was three or four inches deep, and we could tip out the greater part of what was inside.

We looked out for good-sized trees which would be handy for mooring to; such as wouldn't be likely to pull out, like the stake; and we fastened her with the painter, with what was left of the "keleg" or anchor-rope, and with a short spare piece from the locker;—not too closely, but so she could float higher, if the water rose.

Then we took the lantern to light up with in the evening, and some of the spare rope, and started back; Joe "blazing" a path, while we were in the woods, by shaving off pieces of bark with his big knife every few steps, so as to show the white wood, and mark our way straight to the boat in the morning.

CHAPTER XXXIV.

When we reached the orchard, I proposed that we should go on and see how the falls looked. I thought that if they were worth seeing the day before, they must be much more so now.

So on we went, leaving our waterproofs, with the lantern, at the foot of one of the trees, for it wasn't raining much; but when we came to Beames' Brook we were brought to a stand-still. It came rushing in at a great rate, curving across the main stream and swirling up on the farther bank, so that the meeting-place was overflowed for the space of an acre or thereabouts. We could have jumped the brook in plenty of places the evening before, but there was no such thing now.

I had an inspiration this time, and we went back a little way, to where an old rail fence zig-zagged down toward the river, and stopped a few yards from the brink. It was down in several places, and plainly nobody was interested in keeping it up; so we had no scruples about making a raft with the old rails, on which we embarked, after leaving our shoes in a corner of the fence.

It wasn't a long voyage, but we were rejoiced to get through with it no wetter than when we started. The raft was hardly buoyant enough for two; of course we didn't mind our feet being in the water, but we had to balance ourselves almost as carefully as though we were on a tight-rope. If either of us made a step, the affair would sway down under on one side, as though it was bound to slide us off. Then we had nothing but rails to paddle with — the lightest we could get, but clumsy things at best. Every time we ventured to use one, it was at our peril, and we drifted half-way back before we made the other side.

THE RAFT WAS HARDLY BUOYANT ENOUGH FOR TWO.

We managed to land without shipwreck, and soon came to where the water was tearing down the long, rocky slope; we had heard the noise away back to the "forks"; and no wonder. The rocks which yesterday stood out on each side of the stream were now right in it, with the torrent plunging and spouting over them as though it would tear them up and send them thundering to the bottom.

We saw a way by which we could spring from one stone to another till we stood on a rock near the middle; and it seemed really terrific to look up the steep ascent and see that water pitching down at us like mad, all of a foam and splashing up in spray every few feet. We could see up quite a stretch, nearly to the fall; but trees grew across so as to hide that.

In a few minutes we scrambled up there; and its appearance was changed entirely; there was no split now in the upper fall, but the water came down in two solid leaps, with a mass of foam and spray between, at the step. We didn't like it as well this way; it was a show of force, rather than beauty, and the water was turbid and yellow.

We went up the rest of the way, but found no place so effective as where we stood out on the rock near the bottom; and we stopped there again a little while on the way back.

While still in the woods, we cut some saplings to pole our raft along with; the rails we used before were now added to the others beneath us, and in re-crossing we got along easier; especially as we didn't hurry, but drifted down half-way to the orchard. Then we left the raft to its fate, and, gathering our various goods, made our way up to the old house once more.

After giving the fire a fresh start, we went around to take a look at the barn. Here was the lightning's work, sure enough! There was a big jagged hole in the roof, and some boards and timbers which had been torn from the gable were scattered on the ground. They were somewhat blackened; there would have been a fire, perhaps, if that deluge hadn't been pouring at the same time.

Before going in, we gathered a few apples; they were too sour for us in their natural state, but we thought they might be better roasted. Several of the sweet ones which I had in my pockets the evening before had tumbled out when I came down in a heap at the foot of the cellar stairs, and I didn't think to pick them up. No doubt they had been attended to by the regular lodgers, but I had saved the rest, and Joe had all of his; and we ranged them in a circle on the hearth-stones, close to the fire, where they soon began to send out a pleasant odor.

Then I examined the lantern, and tried to see if it would light; but it spluttered and didn't seem willing, so I pulled the wick out and put it back with the other end up; then it burned well enough. I put it out and set it on one of the closet shelves.

On the lower shelf were our "dry goods" which I had rolled up closely and placed there when we started out to look after the boat. As I expected, the upper shelves had kept off the drip, and both blankets and cots were untouched by wet. The sail and tent were still hanging from the kitchen rafters; where the streams had streaked down across them, and they were far from dry; but it didn't matter so much in their case.

The apples were carefully turned from time to time, so as to roast evenly; and when they were done we had supper. Even the sour ones were pretty fair, and the sweet ones were just prime.

It wasn't time for sunset by nearly an hour, but the clouds made it seem like twilight. Before dark we got a lot of wood ready; this time we took all that we could very well get at, wet or dry, for the fire would soon drive out the moisture, and I'm afraid we left the old place considerably more ruinous than we found it.

Our cots were now rigged to swing from the ceiling beams; we drove in the stoutest nails we could find, to hang them by, and arranged the tent and sail so as to keep off the draught from the windows.

As evening set in, we lighted the lantern, and hung it from the ceiling, near the middle. The fire blazed high, with another circle of apples browning and sizzling around it, the cloths curtained us, and shut out the desolate look of the room, and the dark corners. It wasn't half so bad as we thought it would be when we first decided to stay there for the night.

"About this time yesterday," remarked Joe, "we were wondering where we'd camp to-night."

"Yes; and we calculated to be down at the beech-tree. This old shebang was the last place we'd have thought of; we never expected to see it again!"

"Well, we'll have to re-appoint the beech-tree for to-morrow night."

"Suppose it should keep on raining?"

"Can't help it, if it rains cats and dogs; I tell you this place is about exhausted, for us!"

"So I say!" I agreed; "and besides, we want to get home on Saturday, and it can't take us much under two days; we had the current with us all the first day."

"Wouldn't our folks be surprised to see our quarters, to-night? They must wonder where we are."

"Especially if it rained there as it has here!"

"It came from that direction, anyway," returned Joe. "The Holcombs got it as hard as we; and they have thought of us more'n once, I know. I've thought of that wheel of theirs; and if it's stood this, it'll be quite a credit to Tom's work."

"I believe it has," said I; "he knew what this river was before he put it there. You know he told us those posts went down five feet; and there was a sluice-gate, besides."

"'Twould have needed a sluice-gate the whole width of the dam, to let this afternoon's water through. If his dam's stood it, it's done better than ours, it's safe to say."

"Yes; I shouldn't wonder if we'd find a little repairing to do."

The rain had stopped; and the sail began to stir a little, now and then, as a light wind came fanning in. We went out and looked around for a few moments. It was pretty dark; still we could see where the trees branched up against the sky, for there was a young moon behind the thick clouds; and overhead there was a star—yes, two!—now they were gone again; but another was in sight farther down in the north, and the heavy drifts of vapor were flying from that direction. No fear of rain to-morrow!

We didn't sit up much longer, for we wanted to make an early start; we were nicely dried, now, and the apples were done to a turn. Besides, the mosquitoes came in to look at our fire and lantern, and in the course of their wanderings they paid altogether too much attention to us. The nettings were taken from the bags and unfolded; and when I had "turned in," Joe fixed mine so as to protect my head, and arranged his as far as he could without shutting himself out; then he put out the lantern, and climbed into his cot.

Presently a voice came from behind Joe's netting: "What's the name of this camp?"

"*Camp!* in this place!" I groaned. "Don't mention it!"

"Well, what is it, then? You don't expect we've started housekeeping here, do you?"

"Joe, it's a disgrace to the expedition to mention such a thing! Let it be a camp then,— Camp Shebang!"

But that wasn't magnificent enough, he insisted; and we debated two or three minutes, over various suggestions. Finally we rejected Camp Shower-bath, Camp Greer, and Camp Storm-bound, in favor of Camp Dilapidation,— which sounded magnificent, even if it didn't mean it.

Then we found the last night's camp hadn't been named. Joe proposed Camp Thunder-and-lightning; which was ratified at once by a unanimous vote; and we composed ourselves to sleep with a soothing sense of duty performed. I remember listening to the rustling of the vines at the windows, and the snapping and hissing of the fire, while I watched its flickering light on the sail, as it trembled and swayed in the draught, and on the black and ancient rafters overhead.

CHAPTER XXXV.

Next morning I became dimly aware that somebody was talking and tramping about. On first opening my eyes, I was bewildered for a moment by the strange surroundings; then I remembered, and let my lids drop again, saying, "All right Joe!" for I realized that the person I had heard could be no other.

"Joe yourself!" exclaimed a voice which was certainly not Joe's, though it seemed somehow familiar. My eyes quickly opened once more, and saw Ben Holcomb standing by the fireplace, with his face wearing a genial grin.

"So here you are, sure enough!" he went on. "I thought like as not you'd taken up lodgings in this old shanty, when the rain pitched in so yesterday."

"And here *you* are!" retorted Joe; "I *wasn't* expecting to find *you* here!"

"Oh, that's explained easy enough. I woke up before daylight, this morning,—you chaps must find it mighty comfortable here, to snooze this way,— and couldn't get to sleep again; so I got to thinking of you. I knew 'twasn't likely you'd had gone by yesterday, especially in that rain, without stopping to see us;—and we were down at the river, part of the time, too. Tom and I both said you'd likely wait here, for we knew there was no other house within half a mile of where you would have to stop. We looked for you last evening, though; we thought may be you'd come and stay with us."

"You don't suppose we'd have imposed ourselves on you that way, when we were all fitted out for camping?"

"We'd have liked nothing better!" he answered; and, speaking for himself and Tom, no doubt he was right.

"Well," he went on, "I got up softly and dressed, and wrote a little note, which I left on Tom's clothes, and struck out for here just as day was breaking. I took the road straight for this place; and if I hadn't found you here, I was going to follow the river up as far as you'd be likely to take your boat, and then down to our place. But when I peeked in, I saw I needn't go farther; and as you seemed to be keeping open house, I just walked in. I thought I'd see how you looked in camp, and then sail down with you."

"All right," said Joe, who was now up, and starting the fire. "We'll take you down. But this isn't the regular way we camp, of course. We stayed here last night, because we could make a better fire here. How'd your water-wheel stand it yesterday,—is it there still?"

"You'd better believes he is!" exclaimed Ben;

"sound as a nut; the farther end of the dam was washed down, though, as far as the posts of the sluice-gate. We didn't build that part so strong, because there wasn't so much strain there, as a general thing. But the old wheel was put there to stay; the dirt and stones around were washed out more than a foot, but she was planted deeper'n that!"

"She must have spun some, I reckon!"

"No; and that's the funniest part of it; she never went slower than in the worst of it yesterday afternoon. You know she's over-shot;—the trough carries the water right over to the farther side;—well, the water rose over the edge of the trough, in front of the gate, and poured right along into the buckets; at the same time, though it was pouring over the dam against the nearer side in a regular flood, and rushing along underneath, 'most half-way to the hub. So 'twas nearly balanced; but for a little while the stream underneath was the strongest; and she turned slowly over backward, hoisting up the full buckets, and emptying them on the wrong side! Then, toward night, when the water began to go down, she was pretty near still for awhile; just swinging, with the stream spouting and rushing all around, above and below; and later she began to turn the right way. Then the dam kept crumbling away at the other end; and at last that let the water through enough so she could stop. I went down there this morning, and everything was quiet enough. We couldn't drive her even if we wanted to, for our pond is pretty near run out."

"How's the river now, pretty high?"

"Well, some fuller than before the rain, but not much. You won't have any more trouble with our old log bridge; I guess that's down to the paper-mill by this time."

"I should think you'd have fastened it down with stakes or something."

"Well, so we did,—the one before this; but the ice butted it away last winter, stakes and all. We didn't put this one across till late in April; and none of us thought it would need any fastening in summer-time."

"Then it doesn't always rain like this, here?"

"I should think not! I don't know what *you*'re used to, but *I* never saw anything like it, not in July. Sometimes it comes down tremendously for a few minutes, in a thunder-shower; but not for an hour at a stretch. Then, too, it rained all day, and a good part of the night before; I opened the sluice first thing, yesterday morning, and the water was falling over, just handsome, as early as that."

It didn't take long to make some chocolate, and to warm up our baked apples and hard-boiled eggs. "I think likely you're acquainted with the cow this milk came from," said Joe, as he passed a tin cup of chocolate to Ben.

"I think likely I coaxed it out myself!" he rejoined. "'Tisn't so sour as I should think 'twould be, after being thundered at so much!"

What little was left, was sour as milk ever is, I guess; but it was mollified by plenty of chocolate and sugar, and we used only enough to color with.

"I'm sorry we can't offer you any huckleberry pie," said I, "but we cleaned out your mother's pan, yesterday."

"Oh, that's nothing; I get plenty of that, every day. These apples are tip-top; there ain't any of ours ripe, yet. You found them here, didn't you?"

"Yes; in the old orchard close by. I suppose this is the Galloway place you spoke about."

"Yes, this is it; but the people who lived here last were named Somers. That was before I remember anything about it; I never saw it while anybody lived here. I remember it, though, when it wasn't nearly as ramshackle as it is now. Seems to me it's gone to pieces a deal since I saw it last, pretty near a year ago; I shouldn't wonder if you had helped it along some."

"Yes, I'm afraid we have; but we must have a fire, you know."

"Of course! There ain't anybody to care; I've smashed a little glass here myself. Oh! I've been here with fellows, hundreds of times. D'you see my name up-stairs?"

"We did; and Tom's too," said I. "Did you or any of your fellows ever stay here over night?"

"No indeed! It's more comfortable at home. Didn't you find it kinder pokerish?"

"Not a bit; we slept right through; why shouldn t we?"

"Well, there *are* some folks say it's *ha'nted;* — but Tom says that's all bosh, and you can find fools that'd say it of any old house nobody lived in, whether anything ever happened there or not; and father says the same. But there are plenty of fellows that money couldn't buy to come here at night; — not alone, any way."

"Well," said I, "you can tell them that we've stayed here *all* night, and lived through it. I wish somebody had offered us money for it; 'twould have been earned easy, wouldn't it, Joe?"

"You're right!" he assented. "Did anything ever happen here?"

"Not as I ever heard of," said Ben.

"I suppose you've seen that?" I said, pointing to the stanza over the cellar stairs.

Ben burst into a laugh. "I know the chap that wrote it!" he replied. "He made it out of whole cloth, of course; and he scared himself so he wouldn't go down; said he knew there wasn't anything there worth the trouble. He was right enough there, anyhow. D'you go down?"

Then we told him about the pigs; and that lead us to speak of the barn, and how it had been struck; so we all went out and took a look at it.

Ben was quite impressed. He had seen a tree that had been "struck," but never any building.

"I heard that clap; 'twas a ripper!" he said. "Ain't you glad you wasn't in here?"

"Yes!" said I; "Camp Dilapidation was safer, that time."

CHAPTER XXXVI.

The morning was fine as could be; clear and crisp, with a fresh breeze blowing from northwest. We packed up our goods, and left the Galloway place, this time for good; and we were not sorry; though we'd have been a deal more uncomfortable, if it hadn't been there. The pigs were scattered through the orchard, breakfasting on the windfalls; and we picked off the few sweet apples that were still hanging.

When we reached the stream, we turned down along the bank.

"Where's your boat?" asked Ben in surprise, peering about.

"Oh, it's down here in the woods, a little way," answered Joe.

"I should think you'd have brought her clear up, instead of toting your things 'way down there."

"Well," said I, "you know there's a bad place just below here, where the water runs down over rocks."

"Yes, but it wouldn't be any more work to get her up around there, than it was at our dam!"

"'Twouldn't have been, with you and Tom to help."

"That's so!" he admitted.

When we came to the place we'd been speaking about, Joe and I walked along close to the bank, scanning the bottom closely. The water was deeper than when we had first seen it, but it was clear. A little way from the foot of the rapids, I caught sight of what we were looking for,— a fragment of rope streaming down, and playing to and fro in the current.

"Hullo!" I cried, "here's somebody's anchor!" lifting it from where it had caught on a sharp jutting edge of the rock.

"Cæsar! where'd that come from," exclaimed Joe. "Somebody must have been up here with a boat, some time!"

"I reckon so!" Ben burst out; "don't you s'pose I see it all? You left your boat anchored here, and the flood carried her down! You were mighty lucky to catch her again!"

We smiled. "That makes me think!" he went on, "Tom and I saw a pole drifting down, and got hold of it, while we were watching our wheel. We thought it might belong to you."

"I shouldn't be surprised if it did," said I. Our mast washed away, and one of the oars;—you didn't see that, I suppose!"

And he hadn't; but Joe and I thought it was at least even chances that we hadn't seen the last of it yet.

We now left the bank, and made for a certain oak which we had noted the day before, as being close to where our "blazed" path came to the edge of the woods.

"Is she as far from the stream as that?" asked Ben.

We explained that the stream wound about, in the woods, and we were taking a short cut.

We followed our track without any trouble, and found the *Triton* just as we had left her.

"Gewhillikens!" cried Ben, "you meant she shouldn't get away again!"

We untied the now useless moorings, and tipped out the two or three inches of water which covered her bottom; we were glad to see it there, for it showed that the craft hadn't been made leaky by her mad voyage among the rocks and tree-trunks. Then we launched her, and got the freight aboard. Ben was very useful; he had been a great help in bringing our things from the house, and we felt he had earned his ride.

And now at last we were fairly off, afloat once more in our faithful old *Triton;* drifting easily with the current, instead of fighting against it. Ben was ambitious to handle an oar, so we let him shove at the stern.

The effects of the flood could be seen in the woods on either hand; the grass and underbrush were prostrate and draggled, with every twig and leaf swept in the course of the current. Presently a slender pole barred our way, caught by the ends across a tree on each side. Joe easily freed it, and laid it in the boat, where it belonged,—for it was nothing else than our sprit. Now we could spread our sail as soon as needed; that is, if it was really our mast they'd found.

I was splicing the anchor-rope together again. "Tell you, Joe, isn't it lucky the anchor didn't catch till she got to the bottom of that slide? It kept her straight, bows on to the current; if she'd swung around sideways, and happened to hit a rock, 'twould have staved her, sure!"

"Ho!" cried Ben, "so she came down that place! Then you must have taken her up, after all!"

"We never said we didn't!" returned Joe, "'twas you made up your mind we hadn't."

"Well, where did she break away from, anyway? You might as well out with it, now."

I explained that we had intended to "out with it," when he and Tom were together; and tell it to both of them at once. "Though after all, there isn't much to tell," I went on. "We had her moored at the orchard, and after that big rain we went down to bail her out, and she was gone; then we followed along down the stream till we found her."

"And did you find her there where you tied her?"

"No; she was nearer the stream than that, but she was beyond where the water is now; if she'd kept in the channel, she'd have floated clear down."

"And over Odell's dam! I bet you felt kinder uneasy till you came across her!"

"Yes; we didn't know but she'd drift into your wheel and smash it."

"Ho! 'twould take a bigger boat than this to do that!" he declared. "But, my!" he went on, "wouldn't Tom and I have been surprised to have seen your boat come drifting down empty and full of water! 'Twould have looked as though you'd been drowned; but, of course, we'd known better'n than that!"

Here were the stepping-stones; and after we got by, Joe and I took off our shoes, rolled up our trowsers, and waded in to put back the one we had rolled out of the way.

"So *you* did that!" said Ben. "Anybody'd think it was yesterday's rain; I wouldn't bother with it." But we persisted, and soon were able to leave the place as we found it.

"That path leads to Breck's huckleberry pasture," Ben remarked. "I've picked bushels and bushels there; they're pretty much gone now."

We noticed, as we went farther down, that the stream wasn't quite as full as it had been when we came up, although the current was stronger; but this was accounted for by the accident to Tom's dam. We soon came in sight of it, and of him, too, working away at the end on our right. He was so deeply engaged that he didn't see us till we were nearly up to him.

"Hullo!" he cried. "Good morning! glad to see you again. D'you find them where you expected, Ben?"

"Yes-sir-ree! They were at home in the old shanty, all fixed for housekeeping; both sound asleep when I got there!"

"Were you there all yesterday?"

"Yes," said Joe; "the place was close to where we camped the night before; and we thought we'd be more comfortable there, than working along down in the rain."

"You ought to have come here; we were expecting you all day."

"Their boat started anyway!" said Ben, "and got pretty near half-way; but they wouldn't take the hint!"

"How's that?"—and then we sailed in, and told them the whole thing.

"Well! you must have had an anxious time, for one while. 'Twould have been pretty rough on you if she had pitched over the dam below here!"

"They'd a notion she'd smash our wheel!" said

Ben, and Tom smiled; — "but I let 'em know it doesn't smash so easy!"

"Oh, well, there'd been no trouble about that; the main current sets well this side of the wheel. Besides, I was on the watch part of the time, and I'd have caught her for you. I did pick up something that belongs to you, I guess. Ben, you run and get it!" — but Ben had already started for the fence-corner a few rods away; and 'twas our mast he brought back, sure enough.

"It wa'n't no trouble, seeing I happened to be around," he said in answer to our thanks; "I'm glad it turned out to be yours."

And so were we, and no mistake.

Joe got out the pan and bottle, and handed them to Ben, charging him with renewed thanks to Mrs. Holcomb; and he walked rapidly off to the house.

"I'm glad your wheel wasn't hurt at all," said I.

"Not a bit!" replied Tom, with a pleased look; and then he went on with what Ben had already told us. We crossed over to look at it, and everything was the same as before, for Tom had filled in where the bottom had been washed away.

The dam was pretty well wrecked for about one-third of its length; but it was where the ground sloped up to the west, and most of it had been less than half as high as it was opposite the wheel; so it would be no great undertaking to repair it.

Presently we saw Ben coming back; he brought

the milk-bottle filled again, and said there was no need of returning it. Joe was going up to fill our jug with their spring-water ; but Ben took it from him and ran off, while the rest of us got the boat into the stream below. Then he brought back the jug of water, and a prime musk-melon, just picked.

There was a good breeze blowing down-stream, so we spread our sail, and said good-bye ; thanking them for their invitation to come again the next year, and make a longer stay; and we in turn hoped they'd come and see us.

CHAPTER XXXVII.

Off we scudded gaily, with hats waving all around; the wind and tide both urged us swiftly onward, and in a few moments we shot out into the pond, and the Holcombs grew small and distant behind us.

"Hooray! this is something *like!*" exulted Joe, at the steering-oar. The water rippled away on either side, and boiled and bubbled from under the stern; the sun shone brightly on our sail, swelled smoothly out by the breeze,—how different it looked from the woe-begone sheet that hung limp and dripping from those blackened beams, not many hours before!

We went along "humming" till nearly to the narrows; then the woods were so close, they took off a good deal of wind; it would come in a puff from over the tree-tops, and then leave the sail swinging flat; sometimes 'twould take her aback for a moment or two. We didn't bother, though but let her drift; just sculling a little through the narrows, where the wind gave out altogether.

When we got into the lower pond, the sail filled out again. We could see the roof of Odell's mill, and a man working with a shovel on the road just this side of it.

"Guess that's him," said Joe, and he got out his

glass. "'*Tis* him!" and as we drew farther from the woods the wind was steadier, and we scooted along so that in a minute we could see him plainly. He crossed the road and caught sight of us; then he stopped and looked, and in another minute we were there.

"Well, well, boys! so you're back safe, and your boat, too!"

"Yes, and our boat, too!" responded Joe; "but she got away from us once, and for a while we thought may be you'd see her pieces floating along below here."

"Don't say! Where were you yesterday?"

"In the old Galloway house."

"What! in that tumbledown old place? Didn't find it very much better than out-doors, did you?"

"Oh, yes; we made out to keep dry. You've had quite a wash-out here, haven't you?"

The old man was repairing the road, throwing sand and gravel over and among the big stones, which had been swept bare; in some places it was eaten down a yard or more.

"Yes; it was the worst flood I've ever seen here, in July. There's a good heavy wall on the side toward the pond, you see, and a bank sloping from it into the water; that saved it, but for a few minutes it ran over here ankle deep. You see this gangway,"— the little bridge from the road to the door in the gable, at the upper story,— "well, it poured along that and ran off at the sides in a regular waterfall,—all that didn't crowd under the door. At the dam, 'twas clear up to the bridge, and roared so you might have heard it a mile!"

After a few more words, Joe asked if we might go down and get the rollers, to fetch our boat around. But he wouldn't hear of our doing that till we had come in and had some milk; and of course we couldn't very well say no, for he owned the rollers, and we must take them on his terms. So in we went; 'twasn't more than two hours since we had breakfast, but we managed to put away some milk and a generous allowance of huckleberry cake; and Mr. and Mrs. Odell seemed quite interested in our account of our day at the Galloway place. He was especially amused at our laying the waterproofs on the floor above.

"Well, it came near being as bad as that *here*, one time!" said she. "I never worked harder than I did for ten minutes yesterday afternoon, mopping up the water that came in under that door!"

We urged him not to trouble about helping us around; we could get the rollers and attend to it well enough, as it was down hill;—but he insisted on doing so; and as we shook hands with him and pushed off, we felt that no explorers had ever fallen in with more kindly and hospitable "natives."

We had unshipped the mast; for the sail was worse than useless because of the trees, which stretched their boughs above our heads. We made good progress, nevertheless, and easy, too; Joe shoving astern, and I looking out from the bows; neither of us hurt ourselves working, not at all. We remembered what a hot time we had shoving up here; and it was pleasant to feel the difference.

It didn't seem like going back over the same old thing, either; when we came up, we were always looking ahead; now we got the view the other way. Sometimes there would be something we had noticed before; for instance, here was the little brook flowing down from the woods and over the left bank, which we thought must come from a spring; — before, it was on our right. I can say *the* left bank now, instead of on *our* left; for when you read anywhere of the right or left bank of a river, it is always supposed that you're looking down stream.

It didn't seem long before we came to the shoals which had given us so much trouble on the way up. Here they were, but not quite the same; the shifting bed had been washed into new shapes, and instead of half a dozen little channels at this upper end, there were now only two, of which the larger would float the boat and us too. We floated down this nearly a third of the way, before it began to split up.

There was more water flowing than when we came up, and we might have got along by towing her; but that was played out, and without losing any time we jumped out on the gravel and made straight for the dam.

"It's washed pretty well away, I'm afraid, to let the stream get as low as this!" remarked Joe.

A few yards above the dam was a willow, which sent its shoots and branches across so thickly that we had some trouble to get by, on the way up, and we hadn't praised it highly at the time.

It had now done us a good turn, though; for there was our steering oar, high and dry among the boughs.

"Well," said I, "we've done well not to waste any worry over *that!*"

"Oh, I knew it would get tired of going it alone, and pull up for us to come along!"

We left it there for the time and pushed on by; and our dam wasn't quite gone, for we could see a stone or two above water in the middle, before we got there. The stakes had kept that part from going quite as far to ruin, but the rest was laid pretty flat; still, the stones were mostly at hand, scattered along the bottom within three or four yards.

We didn't stop long to look, but stripped and plunged right in, and first set ourselves to filling in the right side and the middle; then we cut stakes and planted them where the water rushed through at the left, and wove our grating as before. The thing was done in less than half the time it took us at first.

"It won't take long for the water to rise to where the boat is now," said I; "in a quarter of an hour we'll be kicking this down again."

As we strolled back to the *Triton*, Joe stopped suddenly, looking intently into the channel close by, where the stream was rippling over the gravel, and over a smooth, rounded slate-stone about as large as my big straw hat. Next moment he stooped quickly over and snatched it up, with one hand at each side,—presto! change! it threw out four wriggling paws with long claws, and a head which shot forth and back so swiftly there was no telling how it looked

'Twas a big snapping-turtle! Joe looked triumphant, and a trifle scared, too; but he hung on manfully. He had caught the beast just right, it stretched its front paws back, and its rear ones forward, but the big claws were blunt, and the legs moved sluggishly, so there was no harm done. All its life seemed centered in its head, which flew out every second with a jerk that shook the whole creature, and Joe's arms besides; stretching around sideways to get at his fingers, which fortunately it couldn't quite reach.

We saw it in a kind of a glimmer, like the spokes of a carriage wheel on the fly.

Joe carried him to the middle of the gravel, between the channels, and set him down. Then we were ready to see him charge at us; and if he could have walked with his head, we'd have had to look out; as it was, he stayed still, with his head part way out, so we could admire his countenance.

He looked — well, dissatisfied; I think it must be harder for a snapping-turtle to put on a smiling expression than 'most any animal. If he could, 'twould be a broad smile. Joe got a twig and held it under his nose; and clip! he had it clinched. Joe pulled up and lifted him.

"Want to try his heft?"

So I took the twig; he was a good solid weight;— more than the stick would stand, for it parted and let him down, thump. He held fast to what he'd got, till we tickled him with another; when he changed for that.

I lifted him by the side, as Joe had done; his claws joined forces and plucked away feebly at my fingers;— but 'twas wonderful how his head plunged out, like the fist of a prize-fighter. He was a thorough-going reptile; more of the alligator about him than anything I'd seen, he had the same saw-teeth knobs strung along the top of his big clumsy tail, and gave out a strange, musky odor, as

they're said to do. His shell opened higher in front than behind, to make room for that tremendous head; it was small for him, anyway; when we poked a leg, he'd have to bulge out somewhere else before he could haul it in.

The water was now gaining;—"Tide's coming in!" says Joe,—so we cut a short, stout stick for a handle, and persuaded him to lay hold. He wasn't as ready as at first; he was beginning to feel that his grip was missing fire, somehow; but he stuck like a good fellow when he'd once got a taste, and we carried him up to the boat, and laid him comfortably in the locker. But first I set him down on the sand, and scratched a line alongside, which was fourteen inches long by my pocket scale,— the shell alone; I didn't try to measure his head.

"We'll be able to exhibit one of the wild beasts of the region!" said I.

"If he doesn't devour us on the road; we mustn't forget he's there when we get out our blankets;— 'twouldn't be nice!"

"The old Romans used to have a sign up where they kept their watch-dogs, '*Cave canem,*'—'beware of the dog,'—so I'll write '*Cave* snapping turtle,' and I took a piece of chalk and printed it on the front of the locker.

"You might as well have labelled it straight, snapping-turtle cave!" remarked Joe.

So we left him in there to meditate; he'd exercised considerably for a cold-blooded animal, and it must have been a new thing to him for it to amount to so little.

CHAPTER XXXVIII.

The water in the channel now began to widen, and, shortly, we got aboard and pushed easily down. We now took our oar down from the tree, which had kept it for us so obligingly, but which gave us a scratchy time to get by it; and the next thing was to demolish our masonry; for the bank was steep and crowned with bushes, so that it wouldn't have been an easy matter to haul around ashore, even if we have cared to do so.

So we moored a few moments, and rolled away the top of the dam; the current was very willing to help us, and it wasn't two minutes before we were afloat again on the lower side, gliding quietly down where we had strained and tugged to get up; all we had to do was to dodge the low branches, and give a shove or two at the bends.

We could see all along how the water had spread beyond the bank, leaving sand and mud on the low, level spots, and bowing the bushes and shrubs in the woods; it had flooded out three or four times the usual width, most of the way. We expected to find that the fallen tree — where the trail led off to the cave — would be pretty well used up, it was such a rotten old affair; but it seemed to be no worse off than before; in fact, it had gained. A lot of sticks and scraggly twigs that had been picked up from a mile back had piled fast against it, and we couldn't go through the passage we had chopped till we had cleared away enough stuff to make a first-class camp-fire; even then it was a tight squeeze, for the water was higher.

After this we drifted gently on; one steering and sculling around the bends, and the other doing little but enjoy the ride. The sun shone bright and hot, but the fresh puffs of the northerly breeze kept fanning us from over the meadows and between the boughs; the grasshoppers and cicadas were tuning up their liveliest, and even the water-beetles spinning and dodging around, seemed to be glad the wet weather was over.

By-and-by was the paper-mill pond opening out before us. We slipped quietly in, and came almost to a stand-still as we lost the current; the distance across was so short it hardly seemed worth while to raise the sail—except to say we'd been under sail on each pond; that was a fancy of Joe's. So he stepped the mast, and took his place at the steering-oar.

Nobody was fishing here to-day; we didn't even see the boat anywhere. There was the tall, red chimney of the paper-mill before us, with the tree-tops clustering around it; and, as we drew nearer, the jumble of roofs began to show above the edge of the embankment.

Now we were close to shore, near the dam; and Joe luffed up, while I went forward and fended off. There were the buildings spread below us, with the rattle of machinery coming out, and mingling with the dashing of the water, which was falling in a thin sheet into the raceway, nearly thirty feet below.

"There's the boat!" said Joe.

It lay about half-way up the bank; there was no need of Joe's glass to tell that it was leaky.

"She went down stern-foremost!" said I.

"Yes; but see! her port side is split 'most to the bow! it's a wonder, though, she held together at all!"

There wasn't a soul in sight; of course there were three or four people, more or less, in the mill, but we agreed there was no need to raise anybody; the bank was smooth turf, and so steep that we could slide her down ourselves; and so we did.

As we launched her again in the raceway, we heard a call, and there was "Charley" in the doorway. We tossed the grapnel ashore, and went over; and while he attended to his work, we told him some of our up-stream experiences. He said the water came thundering over the dam in magnificent style, the day before; and it overflowed from the raceway almost to the mill door; the steep bank kept it from spreading on the other side.

He was looking at the dam at the very moment the boat went down. It sank out of sight, for there was quite a depth at the foot of the wall, but in a few moments it came floating along by, and he rushed out through the shallow water and hauled it in. 'Twas pretty well shaken up, and he thought it would be about as cheap to build another as to try and put it in shape again. It wasn't much of a craft at any time.

"Whose was it,—Jim's?" inquired Joe.

"No; 'twas built by a fellow named Webb. He went out West last spring and wanted to sell her to Tim Conway for two dollars; but Tim didn't think 'twas worth that, so she's been everybody's boat. Guess you're glad enough 'twasn't yours that made that dive!"

The broad band of blue paper was still winding to and fro among the rollers. The long room was cooler and more comfortable than when we were there before, and it was nearly noon when we said good-by to Charley, and floated the *Triton* through the raceway, and past the current that came foaming in from the wheel.

We dropped down around the curves and along the reaches; at last the little house where Joe had set his timekeeper showed its gable a moment between the trees, looking so different from this point, that at first we didn't remember having seen it. A few turns more, and we were gliding through the narrow arch, across the little pond, and winding out over the meadows that stretched below.

The hours of that afternoon passed without anything particular happening; but Joe and I remember it as well as any afternoon of the whole set. We remember the rippling and sparkling shallows, widening into reaches where the surface reflected the tree-tops far above, so that the water seemed to go down as deep underneath, till we got right there, and looked down at the shining brown pebbles within reach of our hands. We remember floating where it was damp and dusky, in the thick woods, with the wind rustling away overhead, but everything still below except for the gurgle of the current where it broke on the stones and logs which lay partly in and partly out, and rounding into bright pools, where the sun streamed down on one side, and made the shining leaves and slender twigs stand out from the shade. There were partly-cleared fields, with clumps of shrub-oaks all tangled and wound together with wild grape-vines, and slender white birches leaning over, with the little kite-shaped leaves all shaking and shimmering on their deep-red switches;—we only had to sit and let them float by. On the way up, we were pushing ahead so eagerly, we didn't take the time, as now, to study our surroundings.

CHAPTER XXXIX.

At last the square-cut ledges of "Camp Luna" came in sight; a landmark which showed that we were nearing Harlow's Pond. We moored the boat, and went up there to stretch our legs a few moments; the well washed remains of our old camp-fire brought back to us our experiments in out-door cooking.

"We wasted near half those fish," said Joe; "another time we mustn't forget to bring the butter. I wouldn't mind trying for another pickerel; what do you say?"

It would be the last chance at fresh-water fishing, and at the rate we'd gone there would be no doubt of our reaching the beech-tree before night; so I'd nothing to say against it, and we cut a couple of poles forthwith. I wondered, though, what we would do for bait; but Joe was at no such loss. He produced a shapeless and tightly-wound parcel, which he unwrapped with quite a show of mystery, throwing off piece after piece of thick brown paper till the treasured contents came to light,—which were simply the heads, tails, and a few other odd fragments of the fish on which we had breakfasted the day before.

"I saved these when I cleaned 'em yesterday

morning; I thought may be we'd find use for 'em." It wasn't a very tempting looking budget, but the fish might see it differently; at any rate, we could try.

While we floated down to the pond, Joe looked over his hoard, and cut off the parts which he judged would make the best show on the hook, putting aside the rest for ground bait. We anchored as nearly as we could calculate to where we had fished last, and didn't have much luck, to begin with; then we hove over the ground bait, and that seemed to fetch them.

At last, when the afternoon was well spent, I got a pickerel bigger than the one Joe had caught when we fished there before;—up to that time we had taken nothing but "'pouts." Now, of course, Joe was bound to be even with me.

Well, he waited till 'most sunset. He said the moon was near half-full, and we had the lantern; it didn't matter if we weren't tucked in by dark,—and he got his pickerel at last; but it wasn't as big as mine. Then he said, "One more last throw!" and he caught another, right off. He didn't feel much more like stopping, then; he wanted to "re-unite the rest of the family"; but I "up keleg" and took the oars, and off we moved, he still trailing his line astern.

The wind had all gone down, and the pond was like glass. The sun was just setting; several of the factory people were out watching us as we drew near. I saw the boy who sold us the eggs, and the other " Frenchies," and there were a dozen or two we hadn't seen before, and a number of men besides.

The first hail was that fellow hollering to know if we wanted more eggs ; but we didn't. Then he was for taking the boat across, and that was what we did want ; but before we could arrange it with the boys, some of the men got to questioning us. We didn't tell our whole story by any means ; but they found that we were taking out part of our vacation in camping and fishing, and had come up from Pierhaven.

Some of them seemed to think we'd better stay there over night, and not try to go farther, it was so late ;—but that wasn't our idea, not much,—our last night out ; and finally they took the job out of the boys' hands, and carried the *Triton* across themselves. And they wouldn't take anything for it, which raised that neighborhood to a higher level, from our point of view.

So we thanked them, and pushed off into the current, which shortly carried us around the bend, and in two minutes we were in a wilderness as complete as though there wasn't a house within five miles. This was where we had such a time working up, and it wasn't very pleasant now, either; the trees were thick, and made it pretty dark ; and they branched across so we had to keep a sharp lookout not to drive into them. Still, it was better than having to force our way up against the current, besides.

We turned and twisted about through this maze, with no clear notion of when it would end, for we'd noted no landmarks along here, on the way up. The twilight was deepening all the time, but at last it grew light again as we came where the trees were thinner. The next thing, there was a big rock just in front! Joe thrust out his oar and succeeded in fending, so we shaved by with a sideways bump.

"Gracious! when did that drop here?" I exclaimed.

"I remember it," said Joe. "It's the rock that had two logs coming to it from the shore,—one on each side."

"Sure enough! and the logs have been washed away."

A few rods below, we came "within one" of running bang into one of those logs, where the river narrowed and it had caught across. One end was under water, but the other was caught in the bushes, high enough for us to run the boat under. The moon was shining brightly, and the trees were rather open at that place, or we wouldn't have seen it in time

"We must keep our eyes peeled for the other one!" said Joe.

But we never saw it; so it must have floated clear down, or else washed up one side, out of harm's way.

CHAPTER XL.

The woods closed in, and, notwithstanding the moon and what was left of the twilight, we couldn't have made out an obstacle more than a boat's length ahead; so Joe said it was time to light the lantern. He was just opening the locker, when I thought of the snapping-turtle! It was so dark, he didn't notice the warning I had chalked.

"Joe! the turtle!" I yelled; "hold on."

He remembered in a flash and jerked his hands back, letting the locker door fall with a rattle. We couldn't see anything, and I didn't know but he'd be sauntering out among us; so I told Joe to shut it again, and fetched the bow in-shore. It wasn't best to have too many things on hand at once, when a live steel trap was to be reckoned with. When the boat was fast, we considered a moment. If we had a light! but the lantern was where he had "the say" of it just now, though he didn't need it,—something like the dog in the manger. But though he really knew and cared nothing about it, the difficulty was to make him understand that we meant nothing personal when we reached in for it.

"Let's light some paper," suggested Joe; "then we can get some idea how the land lies."

So I got out a cracker bag and laid it on the bottom, near the locker, first moistening the boards. Joe struck the match and set the paper going, while I let drop the locker door. We peered in and saw him, with his back turned to us and his alligator tail curved hard-a-port. He seemed to be asleep, but nobody would guarantee that his head wasn't awake, and it was close to the end that the lantern lay glittering.

I thought I'd poke it out of the way, and give him room, so I gently shoved in an oar-blade; but instead of taking it that way, he thought the oar wanted to get acquainted, and met it half-way with such ready good-will that it quivered in my hands.

"His mouth's full, Joe! now reach in for the lantern!"

But before he could get in a position that suited him, the paper burned out.

"Never mind, Joe; strike another match, and I'll get it; he knows me; he wouldn't hurt me for a farm."

Joe lighted a match; but he didn't hold it so that I could quite see, and I thought too much of that turtle to disturb his enjoyment of the oar. So I lit a match, and held it myself, — and jerked out the lantern without troubling him at all.

Joe lost no time in lighting it; and then we thought he'd had enough of the oar, so I tried to pull it away. Of course he thought otherwise;

and when the end came in sight, so did his head, as though the whole thing was in one piece. I don't think lamplight was becoming to him; still, it's hard to tell.

I proposed to shut the door on the blade, and then pull it through, leaving him behind; but Joe feared his jaws would be splintered before he'd give up.

"Let me unlock him; you don't know the combination!"

He cut off the tail of one of our fish, and skewered it on a twig. Sure enough, when Joe began to swab his nose with it, he exchanged, in that sudden, earnest way of his, that made Joe jump. Then we shut him up with his new attachment, and began navigating by the light of our lantern.

Here, where the trees were thick and low, it was curious to watch the changes in the little lighted space just ahead of us, as we floated down. The boughs and twinkling leaves would suddenly grow into shape, and as we passed, they would stand out bright and sharp, every little twig showing up against the solid black ahead; now and then the lantern would light up a branch just in time for us to save it from being swept overboard. Then the darkness before us would grow less deep, and, in a moment, a wall of leafage would be disclosed across our course, with dark gaps between the bright

IT WAS CURIOUS TO WATCH THE CHANGES IN THE LIGHTED SPACE
JUST AHEAD OF US.

stems and trunks below;—then would be a wide black space yawning at one side or the other, all fringed with the gleaming leaves, and we would round the curve into another mysterious stretch, reaching on ahead, we couldn't tell how far.

Then, where the trees were taller and thinner, the moonlight would sift down on the upper sides of the leaves, looking pale blue, after our eyes had grown used to the lamplight.

At last we were in a place which I thought must be one of those long reaches where the young trees arched across; and I had Joe put out the lantern a moment, while I stopped the boat at one side. When our eyes were used to the fainter light, we could trace the path of the water away ahead, by the pale glimmering reflections, and could see the sprays and stems where the moonlight touched them here and there. It hardly seemed real, it was so strange and dreamy; but it wasn't nearly as beautiful as by the bright, warm sunlight. Still it was worth seeing, and I was glad it happened so we could.

We couldn't keep our reckoning straight, things looked so different, so we came on the beech-tree of a sudden, before we were expecting to see it; and it almost seemed as though it couldn't be the right place. But there was no mistaking that great tree; by lifting the lantern we could see the letters cut in the bark,—and here was the little cove opposite. Our cruising for that day was at an end.

Joe had the boat on this last night, and I set up the tent on the little grass plat beside it. We got our camp ready almost as quickly as by daylight. We didn't cook the fish, for the underbrush closed thickly around, and it would be troublesome to find wood; but we opened the lantern and made some chocolate over the lamp,— thanks to the bottle of milk from the Holcombs.

We enjoyed our little supper, watching the spots of moonlight shifting over the limbs of the great beech, while the lantern cast a mellow glow on the trunk beneath. Dimpling gleams and sparkles shot out here and there on the black water, as it hurried by.

"It's going back to Pierhaven," said Joe;—and as we "turned in," both of us were thinking how at that time to-morrow we would be there too.

CHAPTER XLI.

The first thing I heard next day, was the snapping and crackling of the fire Joe had built to cook the fish. I couldn't see the fire, but now and then he would come in sight as he moved about; and there were the great roots of the beech, with the water gliding past, and tall, feathery brakes nodding gently on the bank, all framed by the triangle of the tent-opening, and dimmed now and then by puffs of blue smoke. The sunbeams straggled down among the leaves, and made rounded, quivering knots of light on the sides of my little shelter; and there was a fresh, woodsy smell in the air, with a little smoky whiff, at times, brought by the light breaths of wind.

I lay a little while drowsily taking it all in, and thinking how different it was from the surroundings of the morning before; then I rose, and washed in the clear water of the cove. Joe had cleaned as many fish as he thought we'd want for breakfast; but they weren't all we'd caught so while he was frying them, I set to, and cleaned the others. It was well enough I did, for in the end we cooked another panful. They were just good!

Then the tents were taken down, and the things

stowed away; and we took leave of that pleasant spot, to start on our last day's voyage.

In a few minutes we came to where the rivulet flowed in from the spring; and that reminded us that the jug was nearly empty, so we stopped and went up to fill it. When we came back, we put it in the "fore-peak," where it would be out of the hot sun; and floated along down, past the willowy islets, to the bridge where our young friend was angling for "punkin'-seed" on Tuesday. Some of the planks were gone, but most of the little structure was still in place; there was a bend, just above, which broke the force of the water, no doubt.

The little ferry-boat, farther down, where the steps led up to the gate, was also at its moorings; very likely it was hauled up, when the stream began to rise. We saw nobody here this time, till Joe began to whistle; and that brought the terrier jumping and barking as frantically as before; but the little boy didn't put in an appearance.

In a minute more, we came to the branch we had noticed when coming up, which made away to the left; and we had a notion to see where it would bring us out. It was pretty narrow at first, hardly room for us to push along; but it grew a little wider as we went on, so we could just about get 'round the first bend.

Then the course was nearly straight for some

distance. The current was almost at a stand-still; we sounded, and found it over six feet deep. On turning a corner, we pushed out into a little lake, all hidden away there in the woods. The banks grew higher toward the other side, fifteen or twenty boat-lengths off, and there they were sheer rock, rising from the water ten feet or more. There was a little rocky island, pretty well across from where we were; the half-dozen trees on it were all twined and matted together with vines.

We couldn't make out any outlet, and it seemed we might have to turn back; but first we thought we'd pull to the island, and take possession of it in the name of the expedition. There were plenty of young sassafras shoots sprouting up under the trees, and we pulled up a few of the most promising, as trophies of discovery. As we made our way across, the farther bank of the pond came in sight, and there was the outlet! the island had been hiding it from us.

We got aboard again, and pulled around into it. After several windings, it narrowed; and the bushes grew across so thickly we could scarcely force our way through,— but there was still a current, and it must lead somewhere. It did;— one final push through the tangled vines and shrubbery, and we burst out into the main stream, opposite a growth of willows; and just above we saw two large rocks, with the water coming through between, and flowing around at the sides, too.

We knew it right off, for the place where we blundered about from one passage to another, when trying to find our way up. This time we'd dodged it, and might have before if we'd known how; but the entrance was so overgrown we hadn't noticed it at all; the rocks ahead took our attention. It seems there was a little exploring still left for us, after all.

We cleared the *Triton* of the leaves which littered it after our late struggles, and floated down without further adventure. When the current slackened, we took turns in rowing for short spells; the stream was now wide enough, most of the time, for the oars to be handled comfortably. The water was somewhat higher than when we came up; the way we found that out was by the oar's hitting a log which lay jammed across a little under water, while we were going through a piece of woods;— it was the one where Joe had pitched overboard. The boat didn't touch at all.

A little after eleven o'clock we rounded a low point overshadowed by some large willows, and saw the hill which marked Camp Prospect rising beyond the broad green fields, and looking down on the sheet of water at whose edge our tents had been spread for the first time. When we had seen this spot before, it was at sunset and sunrise; now at nearly noon the shadows were shrunken close under the trees, instead of stretching far across the meadows; and the hot rays beat down from overhead on the bare rocks, and the sandy slope of the wash-out, and on the yellower sand which had pushed out into the water.

"Let's have a swim!" cried Joe, "there's no better place on the river!"

He was right,— the water was warm, and the sandy bottom sloped evenly; it was as good as could be,— for fresh water! After all, there's nothing like the "briny," we were agreed on that. Still, when we swam under the shade of the overhanging willows, and clinging to their tough sprays, lay on our backs while the cool current played beneath and swayed us about, we admitted that fresh water had some attractions of its own.

Noon at last! and, on the hill where we had supped and breakfasted, we ate the last dinner of the expedition, and saw once more, on the far horizon, across miles of air quivering in the mid-day heat, the familiar spires of Pierhaven!

Then we were off again, rounding the rocky base of the hill; and floated without a scratch over the big brown rock we had grazed on the way up. Presently the cool, shady woods were again around us; we were in no hurry to leave them now, but floated easily along, slowly dipping the oars.

In another hour we came to the broad, willow-bordered reach, above which we had seen the first downward current, creeping over the gravelly shallows. It flowed along merrily, now; bearing us into the little pond; from the edge of which a "stake-driver" or bittern flew sluggishly away, so near that we could see the dash of black on the side of his neck. When the stream narrowed again, there was still a decided downward current. Of course we had no objections to that; the tides were neap at this stage of the moon, and didn't reach so far up the river.

When we came in sight of the stone bridge, with its round arch, the place seemed deserted;—nobody around, not even the dog. The boat was gone too; we wondered if it had been washed from its moorings,—but we met it a little beyond, with the same children in it, and a young man at the oars, while the girl sat in the stern. The dog was on shore, alongside; he caught sight of us first, and barked in welcome — or the other, may be,— but most likely because the bark was in him ready wound up, and he was glad of a chance to let it out.

The stream wasn't very wide there, and we hauled our boat ashore and waited for them to go by. We took off our hats to the girl, and she asked us if we found "Shad Factory."

"Oh, yes; we got there all right."

We pushed in again; the dog lingered a moment to bid us good-bye, and then we dashed ahead of the *Kittie Clover*, as she made her way up and disappeared under the arch of the bridge.

CHAPTER XLII.

After an hour or so of pleasant paddling through the meadows, the river forked,—and on the point was Joe's pile of stones, about four feet above water, with the stick still pointing to the left; so the water didn't rise as high as that, when it poured down after the rain. It came more than half-way to it, though; we could see its traces quite plainly along the steep banks. Joe remarked that he thought he stacked those stones nearer the water than that.

As we moved along, we certainly could see the bottom more plainly than when we came up;—perhaps the flood had left the stream clearer than before. We didn't know that there was another surprise awaiting us in this surprising region, but we soon found it out.

There was a faint sound of rippling; and here were jagged points and edges of rock at the surface, and others just below it. These were the same shallows at the lower end of the island, over which we had found ample depth for our passage, a few days before. How could this be, when that same day we had surely found, at places farther above, a greater depth than at the same points on our first day?

"Well; this is the *contrariest* place I ever came

across!" exclaimed Joe. "No use to try to haul over *that*, it'll rake the bottom clean off. We've got to put back again, and circumnavigate this precious island a second time; I believe the river is bewitched along here, after all."

But I saw through it, now. "Joe," said I, "don't you know that 'twas running up-stream here before, and that the tide filled in to 'way above that bridge?"

"Sure enough!" he answered. "'Twas flooded up all along here by the salt water coming in below. I wish 'twas now!"

But there was no use wishing, so we headed up stream again; this time with quite a current against us.

"How's the tide to-day, anyhow?" said Joe. "Let's see,—last Monday it started to come in about five in the morning,—to-day 'twould be five hours later; ten o'clock. If it began at ten, 'twould be high water at four; and it isn't that yet,—not by more than half an hour. It ought to be running up here, now."

"So it would, if 'twas new moon, as it was then. The neap-tide don't fetch up so far, it seems."

"No, that's sure enough; seeing's believing. But we stand a chance of finding where they do bring up. Our down-stream current may give out any time, now."

"There's another thing to think of," I added; "we found it setting up, last Monday, long after it must have started to go out at Pierhaven. 'Twas a regular tidal wave, rolling up. So it may reach even here, before night."

We rounded the point, and floated down into the chasm, turned the angle and shot past the waterfall; there was plenty of depth on this side, anyway.

"Let's land on this wonderful island!" proposed Joe, unexpectedly.

"All right; and we ought to name it, too; let's call it Bewilderment Island!"

"I think Blunderhead Island would be a better name! the way we have bothered and fooled round it!" said Joe.

We made fast to a stout, though stunted, oak, that grew out of a cleft, and walked up along the edge of the fissure, looking down into its dark, cool depths. It seemed deeper than it did from the boat, but no wider; Joe thought he could jump it, but he didn't seem to think it worth while to try. Here came the little stream that made the waterfall, racing down a short slope, behind which it was soon lost to view behind the trees.

This island is mostly rock, all jagged and split, with steps and shelves, big cracks and jutting points. The coating of earth, held together by stiff grasses and tough bushes, grew thicker toward the middle, where the oaks and "pig nut" hickories drove their roots down into the seams, and made the most of the soil which had filled the hollows. The growth was pretty thick for such an unpromising berth, and when we had climbed to what we judged was the highest point, the view didn't amount to much. Even the river was out of sight. We could see the edge of the chasm, for a few feet, but no water; there was nothing to show that we were on an island.

Two or three cicadas or "locusts" were answering each other around us, their machine-like buzz tapering suddenly off, and ending with a few scattered scrapes and catches.

"It sounds as though your Waterbury had let go all holds, and was letting itself run out!"

"If she did, I'd back her to outlast most of 'em!" he answered; "but there's one out this way that kept it up a minute ago long enough to tire out two or three watches."

"I noticed it, too; and it sounded different from the others. Let's see if we can get a glimpse of it."

So we went forward, peering among the branches; we hadn't made four steps, when it struck in again, loud and sharp.

"That doesn't come from the trees,— it's in the grass"; and he turned a little to the left. I followed closely, scrutinizing the grass and weeds. Bump! came Joe into me with a backward spring, and down I went, rolling a little way along the slope, and bringing up in a clump of junipers.

"Gracious, Joe! what in time's the matter with

"NOW," CRIED JOE; AND WE BROUGHT DOWN THE STICKS WITH ALL OUR FORCE.

you,—want to trundle me into the river? a little more, and I'd cracked my head against that rock!"

He said nothing ; he had stopped a little beyond me, and was looking toward where we started from ; I could see he was scared, and no fooling.

"What is it,—a hornet's nest?" and I scrambled up; but I couldn't think hornets would ever have made Joe as pale as that. He shook his head, looked around a moment, and began cutting a good-sized stick.

"Oh, it's a snake!—isn't it?"

"Yes,—it's a snake!" he whispered, glancing up where the cicada had been sounding ; it was still now, perhaps the snake, too, had been after it.

"Well, Joe, if anybody'd told me a snake could scare you like this, I wouldn't have believed 'em!"

"You just wait!" He cut another heavy stick and gave it to me. "Now come on,—and keep a good look-out!"

"I'll look out for *you!*" I returned ; "I'm more afraid of you, than the snake!"

Up we stole cautiously, I keeping out of his range. The cicada started his noise,—and at the same instant I saw the snake! His thick, yellowish body, spotted with brown, was curled in a coil,— and his tail was raised, and all a-whir!

It was my turn to jump, now ; but I didn't tumble. Joe motioned me around opposite, and I crept up within striking distance. The snake's head was on guard, raised and rigid ; and I knew that the snapping-turtle's iron-jawed front was bland innocence itself, to this one!

"Now!" cried Joe; and we brought down the sticks with all our force. The snake shot out at Joe, nearly half its length; he sprang back, and the reptile jerked itself into position again. Our blows had interfered a little, and the end of my cudgel hit a stone on the farther side, so the snake didn't get the full benefit. We let drive again, and hit him fair; and now we hammered away for a minute in a perfectly frantic fashion; before we were half through, he'd had enough.

We were all "beat out" ourselves; so weak· and shaky we could hardly walk straight; but we wanted to get off that island by the shortest cut. We didn't have any idea how big it really was, till we had made our way back over the jagged and slippery rocks to our boat—looking sharp before every step, shaking in our shoes at every cicada note. Joe had the snake swinging across the end of his stick; he only dropped it four times on the way, and we tucked it away in the bow;—and may be we weren't glad to cast off and go gliding down the current, with clear open water all around us!

"Say!" said Joe, "we know what the name of this island is, now!"

And we did. Need I say that to us the name will always be — "*Rattlesnake Island!*"

CHAPTER XLIII.

About the time that the old brick-sheds came in sight, as we moved down, we noticed that the current was getting slower; and when we got to the place where Joe had astonished the cows with the strange tricks of the umbrella, it was at a standstill. In another quarter of an hour, the upward movement could be plainly seen; we were once more within the sway of the salt tides.

Now came the long, monotonous oxbows of the lower river; we pulled around them, one after another, relieving each other at the oars by twenty-minute spells. During most of the day, the wind had blown freshly from northwest and west; but now it was going down. The sun was getting low, and was now hidden by long, fleecy cloud-bands.

"There's the grind-stone!" said Joe, who was then at the steering-oar. But there was now no question of cutting across; the ground was at least a foot above water. The grass was all mown short, and standing about in haycocks; at the farther side of the great bend, four men were busy raking and pitching it on a larger heap at the very edge of the bank.

When we got around there, we found this heap was afloat, — that is, a scow was lying close in to the shore, and they were heaping the hay on it, as they would on a cart; and like a cart, there were stakes around the edge, to hold the hay on. In this way they could gather the load from each side of the river.

We floated along close by them, and they looked at us; one of them saw the snake lying up forward, and of course at that he hailed us; and then we had to stop and tell all about it. Well, we didn't mind at all letting them know we had killed a rattlesnake; that sort of game isn't brought around every day. We were heroes in a small way, for those few minutes we lay alongside that hay-boat; and there wasn't much haying done meanwhile.

They looked the beast all over, counted his rattles—nine—and made more fuss over him than he'd ever had made while he was alive; but then it often is that way. And we knew this was only the beginning of it, too. One of the men said rattlers "useter" be found in that ledge, long ago; but he'd never seen one,—thought they'd all died out, by this time.

At last we pulled ahead, and the men went back to their raking. We went round and round the great bends, east, west, south and sometimes north, till the sun began to dip behind the trees, away up on the western slope. The little half-moon was high among the fleecy clouds, and looked as nearly as might be like a piece of one of them; she was growing brighter and brighter as we came to the fence where we made our first cut-off. We didn't haul

A SCOW WAS LYING CLOSE IN TO THE SHORE, AND THEY WERE HEAPING HAY ON IT.

across at this place, either;—for one thing, we weren't in much of a hurry; for we couldn't get home before dark, now, anyway; and we were feeling rather tired and lazy, besides. When we found how long it took to pull around, we almost wished we had made the short-cut; but any how we got there, and there weren't any more bends as bad as that one.

It was a little past eight o'clock when we floated under the shadow of Wylie's bridge, and out again into the broad river, with our homeward path traced before us by the moonbeams, in a long stretch of glittering ripples. A little breeze had sprung up from the north; we spread our sail, and went gliding along in salt water once more, with our last two miles lying straight before us, and the shores far and dim on either hand. The *Triton* was already at home; this was what she was used to,—instead of pushing through overhanging boughs, and scraping over snags and gravel by day, and staying on shore for a sleeping apartment by night. But she had behaved well; we had no fault to find.

I mentioned something of this to Joe; and he said, "I know one thing;—the *Triton* never dreamed of coming back as a traveling den of reptiles, did she now?"

"Pshaw-haw!" I laughed.

"Well, isn't it so? Alligator astern, and rattlesnake up in bow! Tell you what! nobody else'll ever want to explore this river, when they see the sort of things we fetch home!"

"Well, that's all right,—we'll be the original and only explorers!"

When we passed the bridge, we noticed that the current was flowing downward, and so we had it with us as well as the wind, which just filled the sail. The lights of Pierhaven began to show, and we could dimly make out those final bridges which were the gateway to the well-known harbor. The last train came down from the city; it slowed up as it crossed, a silent line of lighted windows, some bright, some faint; then the hollow roar came to us across the water, and the clouds of sparks rushed from the smoke-stack as they put on steam at the farther side.

Now we began to hear another roar; it grew in distinctness to our ears, as the tall, black, interlocking timbers of the draw did to our eyes.

"It's going it!" said Joe. "Must be about half out."

We'd have thought nothing of it by daylight; I'd often "shot" the bridges alone, but not when the tide was at its most violent stage. We couldn't see, yet, what it was amounting to now; by the time we could, there'd be no turning back.

"It's bright moonlight!" said Joe; "we know what the *Triton* is; if she's stood what she has up there, she can carry us through this. I'll take the oars, and you steer!"

So I rolled up the sail, unstepped the mast, and lashed them securely together; then I stowed them carefully in the boat, went to the stern, and grasped the steering-oar. We now drifted quietly with the current; not very fast, it seemed,— but the railroad bridge, now not far off, was rapidly growing larger and closer.

I pointed her straight for the middle of the wide opening. Now it was close by; through it I could see the farther bridge, with a few black and white figures leaning against the rail;— now we were sweeping under; this was nothing,— the carriage bridge, with its narrower spans, was the tug. We heard some girls' voices exclaiming, above the roar, as we emerged from the shadow,— and forgot it next moment, as we saw the white spray leaping in the moonlight beyond.

But we were in for it. I felt the sharp eddies fighting around the oar-blade,— "Row, Joe, row! and give her steerage-way!" Here the dark passage came yawning toward us; in a moment we swooped down through it on the mighty black swell. Then up shot the bow on the foaming crest at its foot; down it pitched on the other side, scooping up the water; the spray dashed over us, the boat was thumped and buffeted by the white, boiling knots, the oars were jerked this way and that,— the craft was beyond control as we whirled helplessly along!

In half a minute it was over,— we were through. The foam-wreaths were quietly swirling and melting away around us; the roar was far behind, growing less and less; the bridges showed dim and distant in the moonbeams. We looked over our things; they were all there, snake and all; though he'd had a good dash of salt water, like the rest of us.

"I wouldn't have lost that beauty for ten dollars!" said Joe.

There were gallons of water on board, and we took our cups and set quickly to work to bail it out, setting the bags on the thwarts. Some of it must have washed through around the edge of the locker door, and given our turtle his first taste of the briny sea; but he never said a word as to whether he liked it or not.

"Look out!" suddenly cried Joe; "we're almost on Bowers' Island!"

How the current had been hurrying us along! for all it seemed so quiet after we got out of the turmoil.

We pulled around, and passed the island; and just then the bell of the Drummond Mill, opposite, pealed out nine strokes, sharp and clear. Then the clock of St. Stephen's Church, half a mile away in the town, struck in turn, with deeper and slower tones. Another moment, and the heavy Presbyterian bell boomed out,— not striking the hour, but sounding the regular five-minutes' course, which it rang daily, at noon and at nine in the evening. I would know those bells in Chinese Tartary,— was it only a week since we heard them?

We were passing the wharves;— there was *the* wharf; there were people standing on it;— and voices that we knew right well hailed our little expedition, as it drew closely in to the moorings.

I suppose I could take up some more time telling how cousin Albert stuffed our snake as natural as life, and how it set us up among the fellows more than a brevet major-generalship would have done; and how they pestered and "monkeyed" with our snapping-turtle till it's a wonder that some of them are whole yet; and how he got away at last, and no girl on the street would go out after dark for a week; and how long it was after I got home before I got the letter I wrote;— but I've done what I set out to do: to tell how we explored the river,— and I'll stop with that.

I will say, though, that Joe and I have got through with fresh-water exploring, for the present. Not that it wasn't as jolly a week as we ever had; but we like change, and luckily we live where we can have it. So when the *Triton* takes another long cruise, it'll be down the bay, and not up the PEQUONSET RIVER.

www.ingramcontent.com/pod-product-compliance
Lightning Source LLC
Chambersburg PA
CBHW020228240426
43672CB00006B/452